TEST YOUR BIBLE KNOWLEDGE

TEST YOUR BIBLE KNOWLEDGE

1,206 Questions to Sharpen Your Understanding of Scripture

EXCLUSIVELY UTILIZING THE KING JAMES
VERSION OF THE OLD AND NEW TESTAMENTS

Handpicked by Trivia Expert & Nationally Syndicated Columnist

WILSON CASEY

Good Books

New York, New York

Good Books books may be purchased in bulk at special discounts for sales promotion, corporate gifts, fund-raising, or educational purposes. Special editions can also be created to specifications. For details, contact the Special Sales Department, Good Books, 307 West 36th Street, 11th Floor, New York, NY 10018 or info@skyhorsepublishing.com.

Good Books in an imprint of Skyhorse Publishing, Inc.®, a Delaware corporation.

Visit our website at www.goodbooks.com.

10 9 8 7 6 5 4 3

Library of Congress Cataloging-in-Publication Data is available on file.

Cover design by Rain Saukas
Cover photo credit: iStock

Print ISBN: 978-1-68099-355-4
Ebook ISBN: 978-1-68099-368-4

Printed in United States of America

To my daughter, Colleen Adaire Casey,
the possessor of great fortitude—you are my heart.

About this book, author, and inspiration . . .

- The Bible's King James Version (KJV) was exclusively used for all content and research.
- Out of respectful memory, the author used his late grandfather's King James Bible (W. Carl Lanford, b. 1886 – d. 1976).
- Every book of the Old and New Testament is represented within.
- The author's mother, Helen L. Casey (b. 1910 – d. 1980), taught him, "There's nothing more important than being in church on Sunday morning."
- One of the author's favorite sayings: "It'd be a much better world if all of us would realize—we're only here a very short time and just passing through."
- Author's goal for this work: "I am hoping that through my trivia, readers will be triggered to learn more about the Good Book and apply it to their daily lives."

Introduction:
A Wonderful Resource

On paraphrasing the late humorist Will Rogers, "We're all ignorant, but only on different subjects," I, as the author of *Bible Trivia*, want to make you less ignorant about the Bible. Please note that there is absolutely nothing trivial about the Bible. The scriptures are God's holy words as written down by man. This "trivia" work is inspired to educate, reference, and solemnly entertain. But that's not to say we all can't have a little **fun learning** along the way.

Think you know the Bible? *Prove it* by challenging yourself, group, or class with the **1,206 multiple-choice questions** contained within to tantalize the intellect! These quizzes cover the entire scope of the Holy Bible, *exclusively* based on the beloved **King James Version** (KJV). As devised by a trivia World Record holder, these teasers are the handpicked personal favorites. The correct answers include references to the relevant passages in scripture. There's also a **self-scoring system** with lines to jot down notes.

With questions devised to test your divine smarts, *Bible Trivia* contains **201 separate quizzes** with multiple-choice responses. Designed to teach, challenge, enlighten, and entertain, this collection of trivia guarantees hours of stimulating fun for all ages and knowledge levels. These informative questions surround the subject that should matter most in our lives.

This is a great book for **Bible study**. With each question posed, you can look up the verses to gather the fuller story it pertains. This is an empowering and rewarding experience to serve as a powerful base for building and continuing your biblical discipline. *Bible Trivia* is everything a lover of the Lord could ask for and is much, much more than just another *Quiz-like* book in the marketplace. It's a reference guide with a **handy index** to trigger deeper study and understanding.

Respectfully, and may God bless, as I'd love to hear from you via the "contact" at my website,

Wilson Casey
TriviaGuy.com
Spartanburg, South Carolina

PS You'll really enjoy the ease of finding **correct answers**. They're on the same page with corresponding teasers posed. No thumbing to the back, nor flipping around losing your place.

Have Fun! Praise the Lord, and Pass the Trivia!

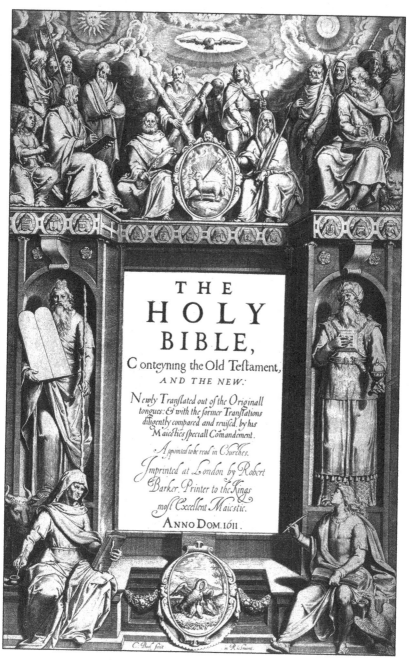

Title Page, 1st Edition KJV, 1611 A.D.

Quiz 1

1) Is the book of Babel in the Old Testament, the New Testament, or neither?

2) In Genesis 18, to whom did God ask, "Is any thing too hard for the Lord"?
   Moses, Adam, Noah, Abraham

3) Before the Tower of Babel, how many different languages were in the world?
   1, 12, 40, 666

4) In Matthew 7, Jesus said, "Ask, and it shall be _____"?
   Cheerfully adorned, given you, asked again, knocked away

5) Whose last verse ends, "Remember me, O my God, for good."?
   Genesis, Matthew, Nehemiah, Hebrews

6) How old was Adam when he died?
   33, 100, 660, 930

ANSWERS:

1) Neither. (Babel was a city in the plain of Shinar remembered for its tower.)

2) Abraham (Genesis 18:13 – 14).

3) One (Genesis 11:1, 4, 9).

4) Given you (Matthew 7:7).

5) Nehemiah (13:31).

6) 930 (Genesis 5:5).

Score Correct_____ Date_____ Name _____
Study Notes:_____
_____

Quiz 2

1) Is the book of 1 Kings in the Old Testament, the New Testament, or neither?
2) Whom did God choose to replace Moses to lead the Israelites?
   Aaron, Jacob, Joshua, Caleb
3) Who was Simon Peter's brother?
   John, James, Andrew, Matthew
4) Which Psalm is the shortest?
   3, 16, 23, 117
5) Per Matthew 12, who is the prince of the devils?
   Lucifer, Satan, the Devil himself, Beelzebub
6) Which of these was not one of the Twelve Disciples?
   Andrew, Bartholomew, Luke, Thaddaeus

ANSWERS:
1) Old Testament. (1 Kings is the eleventh book of the Old Testament.)
2) Joshua (Exodus 17:9 – 10).
3) Andrew (John 6:8).
4) 117 (two verses).
5) Beelzebub (Matthew 12:24).
6) Luke. (He was not there during the life of Christ.)

Score Correct _____ Date _____ Name _____

Study Notes: _____

_____

Quiz 3

1) Is the book of Mordecai in the Old Testament, the New Testament, or neither?
2) Who interpreted the handwriting on the wall when Belshazzar held a great feast?
   David, Joseph, Daniel, Belshazzar
3) Where did Jesus live as a boy?
   Jerusalem, Nazareth, Bethlehem, Bethany
4) How many days and nights of solitude, prayer, and fasting did Jesus spend in the wilderness?
   Three, ten, twenty, forty
5) Where did the Lord tell Jonah to go?
   Jericho, Ninevah, Jerusalem, Israel
6) Which of Jesus' disciples walked on the water with him?
   Andrew, Peter, James, John

ANSWERS:

1) Neither. (Mordecai was the son of Jair and a cousin of Esther.)
2) Daniel (Daniel 5:17 – 28).
3) Nazareth (Luke 2:39 – 40).
4) Forty (Luke 4:1 – 2).
5) Ninevah (Jonah 1:1 – 2).
6) Peter (Matthew 14:28 – 29).

Score Correct_____ Date_____ Name _____
Study Notes:_____
_____

Quiz 4

1) Is the book of Matthew in the Old Testament, the New Testament, or neither?
2) God spoke to Moses through _____?
   A pillar of clouds, a burning bush, a raven, a pillar of fire
3) What tree did Jesus tell unto it, "Let no fruit grow on thee henceforward for ever"?
   Apple, fig, olive, sycamore
4) Who was Isaiah's father?
   Amos, Amoz, Laban, Heron
5) Who asked of the Lord, "Am I my brother's keeper"?
   Moses, Aaron, Cain, Abel
6) Which Psalm begins, "The Lord is my shepherd; I shall not want"?
   1, 15, 23, 40

ANSWERS:

1) New Testament. (Matthew is the first book of the New Testament.)
2) A burning bush (Exodus 3:1 – 4).
3) Fig (Matthew 21:18 – 20).
4) Amoz (Isaiah 1:1).
5) Cain (Genesis 4:9).
6) 23 (Psalm 23:1).

Score Correct_____ Date_____ Name _____

Study Notes: _____

_____

Quiz 5

1) Is the book of 3 Chronicles in the Old Testament, the New Testament, or neither?
2) Upset about Jesus not curing the many lepers, what did the furious people of Nazareth want to do to him?
   Hang him, stone him, throw him over a cliff, drown him
3) In Daniel 4, who had the vision of a tree growing higher and higher until it could be seen by everyone?
   Silas, Josiah, Nebuchadnezzar, Solomon
4) In Acts 12, where did Peter encounter an angel?
   By a tent door, in prison, near the city gate, at the temple
5) Where did Pharaoh and his men drown?
   Sea of Galilee, River Nile, Red Sea, River Jordan
6) According to the New Testament, what is the final place for Satan?
   A bottomless pit, the unpearly gates, a lake of fire and brimstone, Hell

ANSWERS:

1) Neither. (The Old Testament has books of 1 and 2 Chronicles, but no 3 Chronicles.)
2) Throw him over a cliff (Luke 4:16, 27 – 29).
3) Nebuchadnezzar (Daniel 4:18 – 22).
4) In prison (Acts 12:6 – 7).
5) Red Sea (Exodus 15:4).
6) A lake of fire and brimstone (Revelation 20:10).

Score Correct _____ Date _____ Name _____
Study Notes: _____
_____

Quiz 6

1) Is the book of Ezra in the Old Testament, the New Testament, or neither?
2) In Genesis 41, who had the vision of seven fat kine (cows) coming out of a river?
   Adam, Moses, Pharaoh, Abraham
3) In a vision, who was suspended between heaven and earth by a lock of hair?
   Samson, Esau, Elijah, Ezekiel
4) What church did John describe as one with an "open door"?
   Sardis, Philadelphia, Antioch, Smyrna
5) From Acts 10, what was the occupation of Cornelius?
   Fisherman, centurion, tax collector, scribe
6) What little girl answered the door when Peter knocked at the house of Mary the mother of John?
   Michal, Rhoda, Leah, Rebekah

ANSWERS:
1) Old Testament. (Ezra is the fifteenth book of the Old Testament.)
2) Pharaoh (Genesis 41:1 – 2).
3) Ezekiel (Ezekiel 8:3).
4) Philadelphia (Revelation 3:7 – 8).
5) Centurion (Acts 10:1).
6) Rhoda (Acts 12:12 – 13).

Score Correct _____ Date _____ Name _____
Study Notes: _____
_____

Quiz 7

1) Is the book of Gideon in the Old Testament, the New Testament, or neither?
2) Where did Lot encounter two angels?
   A wilderness spring, the city gate of Sodom, the New Temple of Jerusalem, a tent door
3) Where did Jesus turn water into wine (his first miracle) at a wedding festival?
   Bethany, Nazareth, Cana, Gethsemane
4) Who dreamed that the sun, moon, and stars bowed to him?
   Moses, Abraham, Aaron, Joseph
5) In Esther 7, who met his death on the gallows he had built for another man?
   Ahab, Elijah, Haman, Dathan
6) Which is not listed in Proverbs 30 as "little upon the earth, but they are exceedingly wise"?
   Ants, flies, locusts, conies, spiders

ANSWERS:

1) Neither. (Gideon was a judge of Israel. The present-day Gideons International was named for him; the group is known for distributing bibles free of charge.)
2) City gate of Sodom (Genesis 19:1).
3) Cana (John 2:1 – 10).
4) Joseph (Genesis 37:5, 9).
5) Haman (Esther 7:9 – 10).
6) Flies (Proverbs 30:24 – 28).

Score Correct_____ Date_____ Name _____
Study Notes:_____
_____

Quiz 8

1) Is the book of Felix in the Old Testament, the New Testament, or neither?

2) Bernice was the companion of what ruler?
   King Agrippa, Shechem, John Hyrcanus, Pharaoh

3) Who told Hagar, Sarai's maid, to name her son Ishmael?
   Sarai, Angel of the Lord, Abram, The Holy Ghost

4) Per his covenant with God, Abram's land extended from the river of Egypt to the _____?
   Tigris, Red Sea, Euphrates, end of Jordan

5) In what city did Silas and Timotheus stay while Paul went on to Athens?
   Achaea, Berea, Caineh, Debir

6) Who was trapped against a wall by an angel with a drawn sword in a path of the vineyards?
   Baal, Baanah, Balaam, Bezer

ANSWERS:

1) Neither. (Felix was a Roman procurator of Judea.)
2) King Agrippa (Acts 25:13; 26:30).
3) Angel of the Lord (Genesis 16:8 – 11).
4) Euphrates (Genesis 15:18).
5) Berea (Acts 17:10, 14, 15).
6) Balaam (Numbers 22:23 – 26).

Score Correct_____ Date_____ Name _____
Study Notes: _____

_____

Quiz 9

1) Is the Book of 1 Thessalonians in the Old Testament, the New Testament, or neither?
2) Who was the wife of Hosea, taken of whoredoms and children of whoredoms?
   Gomer, Ruth, Sarah, Miriam
3) What servant of Moses became jealous of Eldad and Medad for doing prophesy in the camp?
   Isaac, Joshua, Job, Aaron
4) Who went up out of Zoar and lived in a cave with his two daughters after Sodom and Gomorrah were destroyed?
   Abraham, Lot, Joshua, Elijah
5) Rehoboam took eighteen wives and how many "score" of concubines? One, two, three, four
6) Satan was from the very beginning both a liar and a _____?
   Thief, warlock, heathen, murderer

ANSWERS:
1) New Testament. (1 Thessalonians is the thirteenth book of the New Testament.)
2) Gomer (Hosea 1:2 – 3).
3) Joshua (Numbers 11:27 – 28).
4) Lot (Genesis 19:28 – 30).
5) Three (2 Chronicles 11:21). (A score equals twenty, for a total of sixty concubines.)
6) Murderer (John 8:44).

Score Correct_____ Date_____ Name _____
Study Notes:_____
_____

Quiz 10

1) Is the Book of Tabitha in the Old Testament, the New Testament, or neither?

2) In Genesis 39, whose wife tried to seduce a handsome slave named Joseph?
   Daniel, Shimei, Potiphar, Achan

3) About whom did Jesus say, "For they love to pray standing in the synagogues and in the corners of the streets, that they may be seen of men"?
   Physicians, hypocrites, Sadducees, Adamites

4) In the book of Ruth, which farmer winnowed his barley at night?
   Abner, Eleazar, Boaz, Joab

5) In which book of the Bible do we find the story of Samson and Delilah?
   Judges, Numbers, Exodus, 1 John

6) What man had seven sons who always celebrated their birthdays with a feast?
   Solomon, Job, Hanun, Jonah

ANSWERS:

1) Neither. (Tabitha was a woman raised from the dead by Peter.)
2) Potiphar (Genesis 39:1, 7 – 8).
3) Hypocrites (Matthew 6:5).
4) Boaz (Ruth 3:2).
5) Judges (Judges 16).
6) Job (Job 1:1 – 4).

Score Correct _____ Date _____ Name _____
Study Notes: _____

_____

Quiz 11

1) Is the book of Rehoboam in the Old Testament, the New Testament, or neither?
2) Who was much moved and wept over the death of Absalom, his rebellious son?
   Abishur, David, Joda, Rufus
3) In Acts 9, what woman of good works was also known as Tabitha?
   Priscilla, Naomi, Dorcas, Delilah
4) What beheaded prophet was buried by his disciples?
   Stephen, John the Baptist, Philip, Bartholomew
5) Which book has a verse in its 24th chapter that says children will not be put to death for their parents' (fathers') sins?
   Exodus, Leviticus, Numbers, Deuteronomy
6) What two cities were rained upon by fire and brimstone from the Lord out of heaven?
   Halah and Jazer, Ekron and Gaza City, Sidon and Ziddim, Sodom and Gomorrah

ANSWERS:
1) Neither. (Rehoboam was a son of Solomon.)
2) David (2 Samuel 18: 24, 32 – 33).
3) Dorcas (Acts 9:36).
4) John the Baptist (Matthew 14:2, 9 – 12).
5) Deuteronomy (Deuteronomy 24:16).
6) Sodom and Gomorrah (Genesis 19:24).

Score Correct_____ Date_____ Name _____
Study Notes:_____
_____

Quiz 12

1) Is the book of 1 Timothy in the Old Testament, the New Testament, or neither?
2) What name did the apostles give to Joses, a Levite from Cyprus?
   Barnabas, Cephas, Amos, Gideon
3) Without fear the man who trusts God can trample upon the lion and _____?
   Heathen, locusts, adder, lice
4) Whom did Peter and the other apostles say we ought to obey?
   Wise parents, strangers with good deeds, priests, God
5) What group of people did Jesus say took away the key of knowledge?
   Prophets, carpenters, lawyers, scribes
6) In Exodus 37, who gets the credit for making the Ark of the Covenant?
   God, Moses, Bezaleel, Abraham

ANSWERS:
1) New Testament. (1 Timothy is the fifteenth book of the New Testament.)
2) Barnabas (Acts 4:36).
3) Adder (Psalm 91:13 – 14).
4) God (Acts 5:29).
5) Lawyers (Luke 11:52).
6) Bezaleel (Exodus 37:1).

Score Correct _____ Date _____ Name _____
Study Notes: _____
_____

Quiz 13

1) Is the book of Goliath in the Old Testament, the New Testament, or neither?

2) The Ark of the Covenant was made of what wood?
Olivewood, cedar, shittim, wormwood

3) In Genesis 26, who planted crops that were reaped a hundredfold?
Abimelech, Isaac, Abraham, Cain

4) How many locks of hair did Delilah have cut from the mighty Samson's head?
One, three, five, seven

5) Who made a great throne with a lion standing beside each armrest?
Abraham, Solomon, Joshua, David

6) Where were the disciples Simon (Peter), Andrew, and Philip from?
Zion, Bethel, Hebron, Bethsaida

ANSWERS:

1) Neither. (Goliath was a Philistine warrior killed by David.)
2) Shittim (Exodus 37:1).
3) Isaac (Genesis 26:12).
4) Seven (Judges 16:18 – 20).
5) Solomon (1 Kings 10:19 – 21).
6) Bethsaida (John 1:43 – 44).

Score Correct_____ Date_____ Name _____
Study Notes:_____
_____

Quiz 14

1) Is the book of 1 Corinthians in the Old Testament, the New Testament, or neither?
2) Which Old Testament prophet predicted Jesus would be born in Bethlehem?
   Amos, Obadiah, Micah, Nahum
3) From Psalm 51, "Restore unto me the joy of thy _____."?
   Love, salvation, forgiveness, kindness
4) In Revelation, what falls on earth's waters and makes them bitter?
   A great star, pillars of salt, fire and brimstone, blood
5) What handmaid woman was the mother of Ishmael?
   Tamar, Damaris, Iscah, Hagar
6) Who was the first of the twelve apostles?
   Thomas, Matthew, James, Simon (Peter)

ANSWERS:

1) New Testament. (1 Corinthians is the seventh book of the New Testament.)
2) Micah (Micah 5:1 – 2).
3) Salvation (Psalm 51:12).
4) A great star (Revelation 8:10 – 11).
5) Hagar (Genesis 16:1, 11).
6) Simon (Peter) (Matthew 10:1 – 2).

Score Correct _____ Date _____ Name _____

Study Notes: _____

_____

Quiz 15

1) Is the book of Agrippa in the Old Testament, the New Testament, or neither?
2) In Judges 17, who confessed to his mother that he had stolen eleven hundred shekels of silver?
   David, Micah, Jonah, Esau
3) What animals did Samson use to set the Philistines' field on fire?
   Lions, camels, foxes, rats
4) Mahershalalhashbaz is the longest word in the Bible and is the name of whose son?
   Adam, Moses, Noah, Isaiah
5) What king of the Amorites refused to let the Israelites pass through his land?
   Achaicus, Diotrephes, Sihon, Zeeb
6) What son of David had his hair cut only at every year's end?
   Adonijah, Absalom, Shephatiah, Ithream

ANSWERS:
1) Neither. (Agrippa was the great-grandson of Herod the Great).
2) Micah (Judges 17:1 – 2).
3) Foxes (Judges 15:3 – 5).
4) Isaiah (Isaiah 8:1 – 3).
5) Sihon (Numbers 21:21 – 23).
6) Absalom (2 Samuel 14:25 – 26).

Score Correct _____ Date_____ Name _____
*Study Notes:*_____

Quiz 16

1) Is the book of Zephaniah in the Old Testament, the New Testament, or neither?
2) In Joshua 14, to whom did Joshua give a blessing?
   Jacob, Caleb, Esau, himself
3) What animal did God provide Abraham to sacrifice in place of Isaac?
   Dove, calf, ram, camel
4) How many men in the Bible are named Dodo?
   One, two, three, four
5) What is the collective name of the first five books of the Bible?
   Pentimento, Pentateuch, Pensione, Pequod
6) From Exodus 2, who became a fugitive after killing an Egyptian?
   Moses, Cain, Joseph, Jeremiah

ANSWERS:
1) Old Testament. (Zephaniah is the thirty-sixth book of the Old Testament.)
2) Caleb (Joshua 14:13).
3) Ram (Genesis 22:13).
4) Three (Judges 10:1; 2 Samuel 23:9, 24).
5) Pentateuch. (They are also known as the books of the law because they contain the Ten Commandments and other instructions to the people of Israel.)
6) Moses (Exodus 2: 11 – 15).

Score Correct_____ Date_____ Name _____
Study Notes: _____

_____

Quiz 17

1) Is the book of Vashti in the Old Testament, the New Testament, or neither?
2) Who was the first person given priestly robes to wear?
   Aaron, Abraham, Adam, Abel
3) At the time of Paul being called Mercurius, what did the people of Lystra call Barnabas?
   Pluto, Saturn, Jupiter, Mars
4) "If thou canst believe, all things are possible to him that believeth," are words from Jesus in what book's ninth chapter?
   Ezra, Malachi, Mark, Ephesians
5) In Judges 14, who called his wife a heifer as part of a riddle?
   Saul, Elijah, Samson, Peter
6) Who, along with the other apostles, said "We ought to obey God rather than men"?
   Andrew, Judas, Peter, John

ANSWERS:
1) Neither. (Vashti was a Persian queen succeeded by Esther.)
2) Aaron (Exodus 28:1 – 4).
3) Jupiter (Acts 14:8 – 12).
4) Mark (Mark 9:23).
5) Samson (Judges 14:16 – 18).
6) Peter (Acts 5:29).

Score Correct _____ Date _____ Name _____
Study Notes: _____
_____

Quiz 18

1) Is the book of Zipporah in the Old Testament, the New Testament, or neither?

2) "_____ of the Spirit" is love, joy, peace, longsuffering, gentleness, goodness, faith, meekness, temperance: against such there is no law.
   Belief, fruit, Lord, greatness

3) "Absent in body, but present in spirit" is a popular phrase as found in which book?
   1 Corinthians, 1 Timothy, 1 Peter, 1 John

4) Who was the other man on trial with Jesus whom the crowd freed?
   Barnabus, Barabbas, Pontius, Caesar

5) From Proverbs, "The _____ of the Lord is the beginning of wisdom."
   Love, trust, will, fear

6) Who was Jonah's father?
   Eli, Joppa, Tirzah, Amittai

ANSWERS:

1) Neither. (Zipporah was the wife of Moses.)
2) Fruit (Galatians 5:22 – 23).
3) 1 Corinthians (1 Corinthians 5:3).
4) Barabbas (Mark 15:7,11,15).
5) Fear (Proverbs 9:10).
6) Amittai (Jonah 1:1, 2 Kings 14:25).

Score Correct _____ Date _____ Name _____
Study Notes: _____

_____

Quiz 19

1) Is the book of Uriah in the Old Testament, the New Testament, or neither?
2) What color was the cloth draped over the Ark of the Covenant?
   White, black, gold, blue
3) Who was the first person to go to heaven that didn't die in the flesh?
   Elijah, Moses, Adam, Enoch
4) The derived phrase "whole counsel of God" is found in whose farewell speech to the elders of the Ephesian church?
   Dumah, Paul, Theudas, Timothy
5) In Daniel 4, who dreamed of a tree that reached into heaven?
   Obadiah, Joshua, Nebuchadnezzar, Matthew
6) What was the minimum widow age to be put on a church's support list?
   Fifty, sixty, seventy, eighty

ANSWERS:

1) Neither. (Uriah the Hittite was a soldier in king David's army.)
2) Blue (Numbers 4:5 – 7).
3) Enoch (Genesis 5:24).
4) Paul (Acts 20:16 – 17, 27).
5) Nebuchadnezzar (Daniel 4:4, 10 – 12).
6) Sixty (Which is threescore years, with a score equaling twenty. 1 Timothy 5:5 – 9, 16).

Score Correct_____ Date_____ Name _____
Study Notes:_____
_____

Quiz 20

1) Is the book of Romans in the Old Testament, the New Testament, or neither?

2) When God evaluated his creation after six days, it was _____?
   Heavenly divine, righteous sake, Thine image, very good

3) Who was father of Apostles James and John?
   Zacchaeus, Zebedee, Zebulun, Zechariah

4) Twenty-seven thousand men were killed when which city's walls fell on them?
   Sechem, Sodom, Aphek, Jericho

5) Who made his son walk through fire, burning him alive as a sacrifice?
   Achan, Ahaz, Moses, Shimei

6) From the book of Job, what type of man travaileth with pain all his days?
   Unrighteous, wicked, pagan, oppressed

ANSWERS:

1) New Testament. (Romans is the sixth book of the New Testament.)
2) Very good (Genesis 1:31).
3) Zebedee (Matthew 4:21).
4) Aphek (1 Kings 20:30).
5) Ahaz (2 Kings 16:2 – 3).
6) Wicked (Job 15:20).

Score Correct_____ Date_____ Name _____

Study Notes:_____

_____

Quiz 21

1) Is the book of Samaria in the Old Testament, the New Testament, or neither?
2) What did the people of Lystra call Paul because he was the chief speaker?
   Zeus, Apollo, Venus, Mercurius
3) In which Psalm does it talk about "grease," with the only verse in the entire Bible mentioning the word?
   1, 23, 119, 150
4) Who wrote the book of Deuteronomy?
   Adam, Noah, Enoch, Moses
5) In Exodus 28, what fruit was used as a design on priestly garments?
   Grapes, pomegranates, pears, figs
6) What wilderness did the Israelites come unto between Elim and Sinai?
   Nod, Lot, Dan, Sin

ANSWERS:
1) Neither. (Samaria was the capital of the ancient kingdom of Israel.)
2) Mercurius (Acts 14:8 – 12).
3) 119 (Psalm 119:70).
4) Moses (Deuteronomy 1:5; 31:9, 24).
5) Pomegranates (Exodus 28:32 – 34).
6) Sin (Exodus 16:1).

Score Correct _____ Date _____ Name _____
Study Notes: _____
_____

Quiz 22

1) Is the book of Hippos in the Old Testament, the New Testament, or neither?
2) How does Paul instruct children to act toward their parents?
   Obey, follow, listen, patronize
3) What type of event was Jesus attending when he changed water into wine?
   Revival, stoning, wedding, digging of a well
4) Fill in the blank regarding this verse from Jeremiah: "Can the _____ change his skin, or the leopard his spots?"
   Philistine, Ethiopian, Israelite, Macedonian
5) In Daniel 5, who was so scared his knees knocked together?
   Moses, Belshazzar, Solomon, Lot
6) Who was the first son of Gomer and brother of Riphath and Togarmah?
   Ashkenaz, Jahaziel, Ozem, Trophimus

ANSWERS:
1) Neither. (Hippos was a city located on the east shore of the Sea of Galilee.)
2) Obey (Ephesians 6:1).
3) Wedding (John 2:1 – 10).
4) Ethiopian (Jeremiah 13:23).
5) Belshazzar (Daniel 5:1, 6).
6) Ashkenaz (Genesis 10:3, spelled Ashchenaz in 1 Chronicles 1:6 and Jeremiah 51:27).

Score Correct_____ Date_____ Name _____
Study Notes: _____
_____

Quiz 23

1) Is the book of Zion in the Old Testament, the New Testament, or neither?
2) From Psalms, "The fool hath said in his heart, there is no ____."
   Love, justice, wisdom, God
3) Which apostle acted as treasurer for the group?
   Thomas, Judas, Andrew, John
4) Who got suspended from the branches of an oak tree by his hair?
   Absalom, Darkon, Jabesh, Sanballat
5) What was the occupation of Apostles Peter, Andrew, John, and James?
   Shepherds, tentmakers, fishermen, hunters
6) To which "woman of" did Jesus say, "Give me to drink."?
   Gog, Malta, Samaria, Turkey

ANSWERS:
1) Neither. (Zion commonly referred to a mountain near Jerusalem.)
2) God (Psalm 14:1).
3) Judas (John 13:29).
4) Absalom (2 Samuel 18:9).
5) Fishermen (Mark 1:16 – 20).
6) Samaria (John 4:7).

Score Correct_____ Date_____ Name _____
Study Notes:_____
_____

Quiz 24

1) Is the book of Simeon in the Old Testament, the New Testament, or neither?
2) How long did the waters prevail upon the earth when it was flooded during Noah's time?
   Forty days, 150 days, two years, seven years
3) In Revelation 4, how many elders were seated around the throne wearing crowns of gold?
   Seven, twelve, sixteen, twenty-four
4) Which of these people was *not* thrown into a burning fiery furnace for not worshipping the golden image made by Nebuchadnezzar?
   Shadrach, Meshach, Barkos, Abednego
5) When Aaron stretched out his hand with rod to smote the dust of the earth, what did the dust become?
   Locusts, frogs, mud, lice
6) When the prophet Ahijah approached Jeroboam with a prophecy, he tore his new cloak into how many pieces?
   Two, three, nine, twelve

ANSWERS:
1) Neither. (Simeon was a son of Jacob.)
2) 150 days (Genesis 7:23 – 24).
3) Twenty-four (Revelation 4:4).
4) Barkos (Daniel 3: 13 – 15, 20).
5) Lice (Exodus 8:16 – 17).
6) Twelve (1 Kings 11:29 – 30).

Score Correct _____ Date _____ Name _____

Study Notes: _____

_____

Quiz 25

1) Is the book of 1 Samuel in the Old Testament, the New Testament, or neither?

2) How many years did an invalid lay beside the pool of Bethesda waiting for someone to help him in when the water was moving?
Two, ten, thirty-eight, forty-seven

3) A man was tied hand and foot and thrown outside into the darkness for showing up wearing the wrong clothes at what event?
A baptism, a wedding, a burial, a planting of seeds

4) In Leviticus, who determined whether or not a disease was healed?
The eldest present, the priests, the shepherds, the tax collectors

5) What was the occupation of Zacchaeus?
Publican, tax collector, butcher, merchant

6) What word mentioned three times in the Bible means a "wino"?
Wineslurper, winebibber, graperman, boozejuicer

ANSWERS:

1) Old Testament. (1 Samuel is the ninth book of the Old Testament.)
2) Thirty-eight (John 5:2 – 9).
3) A wedding (Matthew 22:11 – 13).
4) The priests (Leviticus 13:2 – 56).
5) A publican (Which was a tax collector. Luke 19:2).
6) Winebibber (Proverbs 23:20, Matthew 11:19, Luke 7:34).

Score Correct_____ Date_____ Name _____
Study Notes:_____
_____

Quiz 26

1) Is the book of Sadducees in the Old Testament, the New Testament, or neither?

2) In Job 4, who was so frightened by a dream his hair stood on end?
James, Eliphaz, Noah, Cain

3) Where did Gideon meet an angel of the Lord?
In prison, in a field, near a well, under an oak

4) What prophetess of about eighty-four years of age approached Mary and Joseph and thanked God for the infant Jesus?
Anna, Baara, Junia, Phoebe

5) Pharaoh king of Egypt gave what burnt city to his daughter for a gift?
Cana, Gezer, Joppa, Bethel

6) What was the occupation of the man in jail with Joseph who was hung?
Coppersmith, baker, bricklayer, candle maker

ANSWERS:

1) Neither. (Sadducees were members of a Jewish sect.)
2) Eliphaz (Job 4:1, 14 – 16).
3) Under an oak (Judges 6:11 – 13).
4) Anna (Luke 2:33 – 38).
5) Gezer (1 Kings 9:16).
6) Baker (Genesis 40:22).

Score Correct _____ Date _____ Name _____

Study Notes: _____

_____

Quiz 27

1) Is the book of Colossians in the Old Testament, the New Testament, or neither?
2) Complete this verse from Jonah: "And the Lord spake unto the fish, and it vomited out Jonah upon the _____ land."
   Promised, sacrificed, holy, dry
3) What city was beat down and sowed with salt?
   Shechem, Caesarea, Gaza, Berea
4) From the book of Isaiah: "And the cow and the bear shall feed; their young ones shall lie down together: and the _____ shall eat straw like the ox."
   Lion, harlot, fox, slave
5) The wise men saw the star in the _____?
   North, South, East, West
6) On what mountain did Elijah challenge the prophets of Baal?
   Zion, Horeb, Pisgah, Carmel

ANSWERS:

1) New Testament. (Colossians is the twelfth book of the New Testament.)
2) Dry (Jonah 2:10).
3) Shechem (Judges 9:41 – 45).
4) Lion (Isaiah 11:7).
5) East (Matthew 2:1 – 2).
6) Carmel (1 Kings 18:19 – 25).

Score Correct_____ Date_____ Name _____

Study Notes:_____

_____

Quiz 28

1) Is the book of Psalms in the Old Testament, the New Testament, or neither?

2) Whose vision in Revelation saw the souls of God's martyrs underneath the altar?
   John, Isaiah, Ezekiel, Daniel

3) Who baptized the Ethiopian eunuch, a foreign dignitary?
   John the Baptist, Philip, Peter, Jesus

4) What's the only Jesus miracle reported in all four gospels of the New Testament?
   Turning water into wine, the feeding of the five thousand, raising Lazarus from the dead, parting the Red Sea

5) In Judges 9, who had seventy of his brothers killed on one stone?
   Belshazzar, Naboth, Hanun, Abimelech

6) The Ark of the Covenant was carried around what city once a day for seven days?
   Ramah, Moroni, Jericho, Hebron

ANSWERS:

1) Old Testament. (Psalms is the nineteenth book of the Old Testament.)

2) John (Author of the book of Revelation. Revelation 6:9).

3) Philip (Acts 8:27, 34 – 38).

4) The feeding of the five thousand (Matthew 14:13 – 21; Mark 6:30 – 44; Luke 9:10 – 17; John 6:1 – 15).

5) Abimelech (Judges 9:16 – 18, 56).

6) Jericho (Joshua 6:1 – 15).

Score Correct _____ Date_____ Name _____

Study Notes: _____

_____

Quiz 29

1) Is the book of Carmel in the Old Testament, the New Testament, or neither?

2) "Armageddon," the prophesied location of a gathering of armies for a battle during the end times, is specifically mentioned how many times in the Bible?
Once, twice, seven times, thirteen times

3) At what city's public bonfire were books worth fifty thousand pieces of silver burned?
Ephesus, Derbe, Perga, Lystra

4) In Exodus 34, who, along with all the children of Israel, was frightened of a man who came down a mountain with a shining face?
Laban, Stephen, Aaron, Cornelius

5) In what color did king Solomon have his carriage upholstered?
Gold, white, red, purple

6) Fill in the blank: "There was a man in the land of _____, whose name was Job."
Oz, Uz, Ed, Ai

ANSWERS:

1) Neither. (Carmel is a coastal mountain range in northern Israel.)
2) Once (Revelation 16:16).
3) Ephesus (Acts 19:17 – 19).
4) Aaron (Exodus 34:29 – 30).
5) Purple (Song of Solomon 3:9 – 10).
6) Uz (Job 1:1).

Score Correct_____ Date_____ Name _____
Study Notes:_____
_____

Quiz 30

1) Is the book of Bethlehem in the Old Testament, the New Testament, or neither?
2) 2 Corinthians 5:17 focuses on what that could be reasonably interpreted as an upcoming new year?
   Blessings, new creature, grace, church attendance
3) In the book of Matthew, who told Joseph (in a dream) the baby's name was to be Jesus?
   An angel, Mary, an innkeeper, the magi
4) Who, along with his wife Sapphira three hours later, fell dead after lying about a property deal?
   Nehemiah, Shimei, Levi, Ananias
5) Zipporah was whose wife?
   No one, Moses, Andrew, Paul
6) Who used sorcery and bewitched the people of Samaria before becoming baptized?
   Esrom, Hushah, Jambres, Simon

ANSWERS:
1) Neither. (Bethlehem is a town in Palestine where Jesus was born.)
2) New creature (2 Corinthians 5:17).
3) Angel (Matthew 1:20 – 21).
4) Ananias (Acts 5:1 – 10).
5) Moses (Exodus 18:2).
6) Simon (Acts 8:9 – 13).

Score Correct_____ Date_____ Name _____
Study Notes: _____
_____

Quiz 31

1) Is the book of Delilah in the Old Testament, the New Testament, or neither?
2) Which of these names does not appear in the Bible?
   Jada, Justin, Jahaziah, Jahdo
3) In Esther 7, who met his death on gallows he built for another man (Mordecai)?
   Herod, Haman, Jehu, Ezekiel
4) What charioteer rode to Jezreel to find king Joram?
   Jehu, Omri, Naboth, Jethro
5) Who was Belteshazzar better known as?
   Satan, Daniel, James, Goliath
6) Fill in the blank from the Lord's Prayer, "Our Father which art in heaven, _____ be thy name".
   Blessed, forever, hallowed, Jehovah

ANSWERS:

1) Neither. (Delilah is best remembered as the woman who betrayed Samson.)
2) Justin (Jada: 1 Chronicles 2:28, Jahaziah: Ezra 10:15, Jahdo: 1 Chronicles 5:14).
3) Haman (Esther 7:9 – 10).
4) Jehu (2 Kings 9:15 – 16).
5) Daniel (Daniel 1:7).
6) Hallowed (Matthew 6:9, Luke 11:2).

Score Correct_____ Date_____ Name _____
Study Notes:_____
_____

Quiz 32

1) Is the book of Elam in the Old Testament, the New Testament, or neither?
2) Is the phrase "sea monsters" specifically referred to in the Bible, and if so, where?
   Of course not, Lamentations 4:3, Isaiah 20:2, Revelation 6:6
3) Who should be sober, grave, sound in faith, in charity, in patience?
   Tillers of the field, aged men, worshippers, soldiers
4) Who was called gluttonous and a winebibber?
   The Son of man, Nahor, Judas, Nebuchadnezzar
5) What did the bride in Song of Solomon compare her husband's eyes to?
   Owls, cats, serpents, doves
6) Who was the son of Maaseiah and father of Baruch and Seraiah?
   Neriah, Shagee, Shebna, Zalmunna

ANSWERS:

1) Neither. (Elam was a son of Shem.)
2) Lamentations 4:3 (Isaiah 27:1 refers to leviathan the dragon in the sea, also Job 41:1, Psalm 74:14, and Psalm 104:26).
3) Aged men (Titus 2:1 – 2).
4) The Son of man (Matthew 11:19).
5) Doves (Song of Solomon 1:15).
6) Neriah (Jeremiah 32:12, 51:59).

Score Correct_____ Date_____ Name _____
Study Notes:_____
_____

Quiz 33

1) Is the book of Euphrates in the Old Testament, the New Testament, or neither?

2) Who must be grave, not doubletongued, not given to much wine, not greedy of filthy lucre?
   Lovers of the Lord, apostles, deacons, tax collectors

3) The Ten Commandments are found in which two books of the Bible?
   Genesis and Leviticus, Exodus and Deuteronomy, Joshua and Judges, Numbers and Ruth

4) What does James state is an unruly evil, full of poison?
   An unholy wife, lust, the tongue, vengeance

5) Which is not one of the mountains Solomon calls his spouse to the top of?
   Amana, Shenir, Hermon, Zion

6) From Galatians, the law came how many years later after Abraham?
   1, 50, 100, 430

ANSWERS:

1) Neither. (Euphrates is a river in Mesopotamia.)
2) Deacons (1 Timothy 3:8).
3) Exodus and Deuteronomy (Exodus 20:1 – 17; Deuteronomy 5:4 – 21).
4) The tongue (James 3:8).
5) Zion (Song of Solomon 4:8).
6) 430 (Galatians 3:16 – 18).

Score Correct _____ Date _____ Name _____
Study Notes: _____
_____

Quiz 34

1) Is the book of Goshen in the Old Testament, the New Testament, or neither?
2) How far did Joseph and Mary travel before they realized the twelve-year-old Jesus was missing, as he tarried behind in Jerusalem?
   Forty steps, two furlongs, one mile, a day's journey
3) Where did Solomon have a vineyard?
   Ashdod, Baalhamon, Kabzeel, Parthia
4) Just as Moses lifted up _____ in the desert, so the Son of man must be lifted up, that everyone who believes in him may have eternal life?
   His staff, the serpent, his flock, his eyes
5) From the book of Genesis, Melchizedek was king of what city?
   Beit El, Jabesh-Gilead, Salem, Tel Megiddo
6) Fill in the blank to the popular scripture verse, "For God so loved the world, that he gave his only begotten Son, that whosoever believeth in him should not perish, but have _____ life."
   Meaningful, eternal, second, everlasting

ANSWERS:
1) Neither. (Goshen was a district in Egypt where Jacob and his family settled.)
2) A day's journey (Luke 2:42 – 44).
3) Baalhamon (Song of Solomon 8:11).
4) The serpent (John 3:14 – 15).
5) Salem (Genesis 14:18).
6) Everlasting (John 3:16).

Score Correct _____ Date _____ Name _____

Study Notes: _____

_____

Quiz 35

1) Is the book of Haggai in the Old Testament, the New Testament, or neither?
2) From Isaiah, the Lord saith "though your sins be red like crimson, they shall be as _____"?
   Wool, manna, clouds, water
3) Who is credited with being "Mother of all living"?
   Ruth, Sarah, Eve, Esther
4) Methuselah lived 969 years, Jared lived 962 years, Noah was third at 950, and who was the fourth-oldest, living 930 years?
   Abiel, Adam, Enos, Rezon
5) What city in Cilicia was Paul the Apostle born?
   Beth-Zur, Tarsus, Secacah, Ezion-Geber
6) In Numbers 22, to whom did the ass (donkey) speak to?
   Silas, Daniel, Jeremiah, Balaam

ANSWERS:

1) Old Testament. (Haggai is the thirty-seventh book of the Old Testament.)
2) Wool (Isaiah 1:18).
3) Eve (Genesis 3:20).
4) Adam (Genesis 5:27, 5:20, 9:29, 5:5).
5) Tarsus (Acts 21:39).
6) Balaam (Numbers 22:28 – 30).

Score Correct _____ Date _____ Name _____
Study Notes: _____
_____

Jacob Wrestles With an Angel

Quiz 36

1) Is the book of Esau in the Old Testament, the New Testament, or neither?
2) Which of these cities was not cursed by Jesus?
   Chorazin, Bethsaida, Capernaum, Damascus
3) Who was Jacob's firstborn?
   Reuben, Ehud, Joshua, Elah
4) When there was war at Gath, there was a man of great stature who had how many fingers on each hand and how many toes on each foot?
   Four, six, eight, ten
5) Who is not the author of confusion, but of peace, as Paul proclaims?
   God, Paul (himself), Matthew, Luke
6) From Proverbs, what is rather to be chosen than great riches?
   Good name, loving mate, tranquility, restraint

ANSWERS:
1) Neither. (Esau was a cunning hunter and son of Isaac.)
2) Damascus (Matthew 11:20 – 24; the other three rejected Jesus and did not repent).
3) Reuben (Genesis 35:23).
4) Six (1 Chronicles 20:6).
5) God (1 Corinthians 14:33).
6) Good name (Proverbs 22:1).

Score Correct _____ Date _____ Name _____

Study Notes: _____

_____

Quiz 37

1) Is the book of Hyssop in the Old Testament, the New Testament, or neither?

2) Regarding the telling of lies, what are abomination to the Lord?
False witnesses, deceitful voices, failing thoughts, lying lips

3) From Ephesians, what are we saved through?
Forgiveness, following, faith, friendship

4) Who died giving birth to Benoni, who was later renamed Benjamin by his father Jacob?
Rachel, Bathshua, Leah, Jael

5) God is not a _____ in that he should repent?
Deceiver, man, spirit, teacher

6) In 2 Chronicles, who was the eight-year-old boy that reigned in Jerusalem for three months and ten days?
Shamgar, Jehoiachin, Adino, Sisera

ANSWERS:

1) Neither. (Hyssop is an herb with cleansing, medicinal, and flavoring properties.)

2) Lying lips (Proverbs 12:22).

3) Faith (Ephesians 2:8 – 9).

4) Rachel (Genesis 35:15 – 18).

5) Man (Numbers 23:19).

6) Jehoiachin (2 Chronicles 36:9. Note: 2 Kings 24:8 has him as eighteen, not eight).

Score Correct _____ Date_____ Name _____

Study Notes: _____

_____

Quiz 38

1) Is the book of 1 John in the Old Testament, the New Testament, or neither?
2) Whom did the Lord speak unto face to face, as a man speaketh unto his friend?
   Adam, Eve, Enoch, Moses
3) In 2 Kings, how old was Ahaziah when he began to reign in Jerusalem?
   Eight, twelve, eighteen, twenty-two
4) Fill in the blank: "But Jesus beheld them, and said unto them, with men this is impossible; but with God all things are _____."
   Doable, magnificent, possible, thriving
5) Habakkuk says people are ordained for judgment and the Lord has established them for what?
   Warring ways, correction, worship, kindness
6) When the Israelites complained of not having any meat, what did God provide so much that they were buried in them?
   Fishes, quails, hares, chickens

ANSWERS:
1) New Testament. (1 John is the twenty-third book of the New Testament.)
2) Moses (Exodus 33:11).
3) Twenty-two (2 Kings 8:26. Note: 2 Chronicles 22:2 has him at forty-two, not twenty-two).
4) Possible (Matthew 19:26).
5) Correction (Habakkuk 1:12).
6) Quails (Numbers 11:31).

Score Correct_____ Date_____ Name _____
Study Notes:_____

Quiz 39

1) Is the book of Herod in the Old Testament, the New Testament, or neither?
2) In 1 Kings, how many stalls did Solomon have for his horses and chariots?
   One hundred, one thousand, ten thousand, forty thousand
3) Habakkuk says that the just will live by his _____?
   Means, faith, wits, worship
4) The preacher in the book of Ecclesiastes said of making many books, there is no _____ as much study is a weariness of the flesh?
   Value, end, hope, knowledge
5) Who was Ahi the son of?
   Abdiel, Ardon, Aretas, Ashbel
6) What is the last word of the Old Testament, "Lest I come and smite the earth with a _____."?
   Flood, fire, famine, curse

ANSWERS:

1) Neither. (Among the various Herods was "Herod the Great," who sought to kill Jesus.)
2) Forty thousand (1 Kings 4:26. Note: 2 Chronicles 9:25 says four thousand, not forty).
3) Faith (Habakkuk 2:4).
4) End (Ecclesiastes 12:12).
5) Abdiel (1 Chronicles 5:15).
6) Curse (Malachi 4:6).

Score Correct_____ Date_____ Name _____
Study Notes: _____

_____

Quiz 40

1) Is the book of Joanna in the Old Testament, the New Testament, or neither?

2) Who were in Mizpah, where Samuel had them fasting because of their idolatry?
   Israelites, Macedonians, Libyans, Persians

3) How many years did Solomon reign in Jerusalem over all Israel?
   Seven, twenty-two, thirty-one, forty

4) Who was the chief deity of the Philistines, represented as a half-man, half-fish creature?
   Bullock, Elohim, Dagon, Baal-gad

5) Who slew a giant that had six fingers on each hand and six toes on each foot?
   Sibbechai, Cyrus, Silas, Jonathan

6) What tribe was not numbered among the children of Israel, as the Lord commanded Moses?
   Naphtali, Levites, Asher, Manasseh

ANSWERS:

1) Neither. (Joanna was a disciple of Jesus and friend of Mary Magdalene.)

2) Israelites (1 Samuel 7:3 – 6).

3) Forty (2 Chronicles 9:30).

4) Dagon (Judges 16:23).

5) Jonathan (2 Samuel 21:20 – 21).

6) Levites (Numbers 2:33).

Score Correct_____ Date_____ Name _____
*Study Notes:*_____
_____

Quiz 41

1) Is the book of Jehoshaphat in the Old Testament, the New Testament, or neither?

2) The word of God is quick, and powerful, and sharper than any?
   Tongue, knife, two-edged sword, wit

3) In 1 Samuel, whose voice did Samuel think it was when he first heard God calling him?
   Jonathan, Saul, Ahiah, Eli

4) How many chosen men of Israel did Saul take with him to the wilderness of Ziph to search for David?
   Twelve, one hundred, two hundred, three thousand

5) In Genesis 26, where did Isaac stay when there was a famine in the land?
   Gerar, Endor, Sychar, Lydda

6) What insect was a plague on the Egyptians that ate every herb of the land?
   Wasps, locusts, ants, cockroaches

ANSWERS:

1) Neither. (There are several Jehoshaphats in the scriptures, including a king of Judah.)

2) Two-edged sword (Hebrews 4:12).

3) Eli (1 Samuel 3:4 – 8).

4) Three thousand (1 Samuel 26:2).

5) Gerar (Genesis 26:1).

6) Locusts (Exodus 10:12 – 14).

Score Correct _____ Date_____ Name _____
Study Notes: _____
_____

Quiz 42

1) Is the book of Benjamin in the Old Testament, the New Testament, or neither?

2) Who said, "John indeed baptized with water; but ye shall be baptized with the Holy Ghost."?
Matthew, Mark, John the Baptist, Jesus

3) Jesus says that you have to do what to see the kingdom of God?
Love one another, be born again, do what's right, tithe

4) In Leviticus 14, how long was a "clean" person required to remain outside his tent?
One night, two nights, four days, seven days

5) Which apostle's mother-in-law was referred to as being taken with a great fever?
Simon (Peter), Judas, James, Andrew

6) What town or city was Saul of Tarsus near when he converted to Christianity?
Damascus, Assos, Corinth, Gaza

ANSWERS:

1) Neither. (Benjamin, youngest son of Jacob, was progenitor of the Israelite Tribe of Benjamin.)

2) Jesus (Acts 11:16).

3) Be born again (John 3:3).

4) Seven days (Leviticus 14:8).

5) Simon (Peter) (Luke 4:38 – 40).

6) Damascus (Acts 9:3 – 6).

Score Correct_____ Date_____ Name _____
Study Notes:_____
_____

Quiz 43

1) Is the book of Daniel in the Old Testament, the New Testament, or neither?

2) In Genesis 3, who made coats (clothes) for Adam and Eve out of skins?
   Adam, Eve, The Lord, Serpent

3) What did Jesus say his followers would never walk in?
   Fear, solitude, darkness, shame

4) Lamentations 3 speaks of the wormwood and the _____?
   Tree, gall, fence, fig

5) Who had a vision of a lion that had eagle's wings?
   John the Baptist, Peter, Herod, Daniel

6) In 2 Samuel, who killed Amasa?
   Joab, Sheba, Abishai, Bichri

ANSWERS:

1) Old Testament. (Daniel is the twenty-seventh book of the Old Testament.)

2) The Lord (Genesis 3:21).

3) Darkness (John 8:12).

4) Gall (Lamentations 3:19).

5) Daniel (Daniel 7:2 – 4).

6) Joab (2 Samuel 20:9 – 10).

Score Correct_____ Date_____ Name _____

Study Notes: _____

_____

Quiz 44

1) Is the book of Balaam in the Old Testament, the New Testament, or neither?

2) In Titus 1, Paul wrote, "Unto the pure all things are _____"?
   Gold, righteous, worthy, pure

3) What archangel is clearly called by name in the book of Jude?
   Gabriel, Silas, Michael, Melchizedek

4) In 1 Kings 21, who forbade Naboth to give his vineyard to Ahab?
   The Lord, Jezebel, Absalom, Balaam

5) The word "soap" is only specifically mentioned how many times in the Bible?
   One, two, three, four

6) In Psalm 103, what bird's youth is renewable?
   Dove, eagle, raven, swallow

ANSWERS:

1) Neither. (Balaam was the man an ass [donkey] spoke to in Numbers 22.)

2) Pure (Titus 1:15).

3) Michael (Jude 1:9).

4) The Lord (1 Kings 21:2 – 3).

5) Two (Jeremiah 2:22, Malachi 3:2. Called snow water in Job 9:30).

6) Eagle (Psalm 103:5).

Score Correct_____ Date_____ Name _____

Study Notes: _____

_____

Quiz 45

1) Is the book of Caleb in the Old Testament, the New Testament, or neither?
2) Which is not one of the three angels mentioned by name in the Bible?
   Michael, Raphael, Lucifer, Gabriel
3) What king wrote a letter to Hezekiah concerning surrender?
   Sennacherib, Artaxerxes, Belshazzar, Jabin
4) When God took one of Adam's ribs to create Eve, what was Adam doing?
   Eating fruits, shunning away the serpent, sleeping, talking with God
5) What did Barnabas sell so he could lay money at the apostles' feet?
   Manservant, an ass (donkey), his house, land
6) As part of a ritual atonement, what was the goat called that carried sins away from the camp?
   Agew, billy, scapegoat, Verata

ANSWERS:

1) Neither. (Caleb was a son of Jephunneh.)
2) Raphael (Raphael is mentioned in the Book of Tobit, but not in KJV Bibles).
3) Sennacherib (2 Kings 19:14—16).
4) Sleeping (Genesis 2:21).
5) Land (Acts 4:36 – 37).
6) Scapegoat (Leviticus 16:10).

Score Correct _____ Date _____ Name _____
Study Notes: _____

_____

Quiz 46

1) Is the book of Deuteronomy in the Old Testament, the New Testament, or neither?

2) Who said, "The harvest truly *is* plenteous, but the labourers *are* few"?
Cain, Noah, Elisha, Jesus

3) How many total children did Rehoboam have with his eighteen wives and sixty concubines?
Zero, one, eighteen, eighty-eight

4) In Acts 7, Jacob sent people to Egypt when he heard what was there?
Water, work, corn, housing

5) Who ought to be the first to receive his share of the fruits (crops)?
The priest, the husbandman, the eldest son, the sickly

6) Who was the sister of Moses and Aaron?
Ruth, Miriam, Abigail, Hephzibab

ANSWERS:

1) Old Testament. (Deuteronomy is the fifth book of the Old Testament.)
2) Jesus (Matthew 9:37).
3) Eighty-eight (2 Chronicles 11:21).
4) Corn (Acts 7:12).
5) The husbandman [farmer] (2 Timothy 2:6).
6) Miriam (Exodus 15:20, Numbers 26:59).

Score Correct_____ Date_____ Name _____
Study Notes:_____
_____

Quiz 47

1) Is the book of 1 Chronicles in the Old Testament, the New Testament, or neither?

2) To see Jesus, Zacchaeus, who was chief among the publicans, climbed what type of tree?
   Fig, carob, sycomore, box

3) From which gospel does Jesus say the scripture cannot be broken?
   Matthew, Mark, Luke, John

4) In Matthew 17, what did Peter find with a piece of money in its mouth?
   Ram, fish, viper, raven

5) Who were surnamed Boanerges, which is "The Sons of Thunder"?
   James and John, Thomas and Judas, Peter and Andrew, Philip and Matthew

6) Jesus caused swine to rush into what body of water?
   River Jordan, Dead Sea, Nile River, Sea of Galilee

ANSWERS:

1) Old Testament. (1 Chronicles is the thirteenth book of the Old Testament.)

2) Sycomore (Luke 19:2 – 4).

3) John (John 10:35).

4) Fish (Matthew 17:26 – 27).

5) James and John (Mark 3:17).

6) Sea of Galilee (Luke 8:26, 32 – 33).

Score Correct _____ Date _____ Name _____

Study Notes: _____

_____

Quiz 48

1) Is the book of Edom in the Old Testament, the New Testament, or neither?
2) Who hid two spies on the roof of a harlot's house?
   Hosea, Ezra, Satan, Rahab
3) Which book begins, "Now it came to pass in the thirtieth year . . . that the heavens were opened, and I saw visions of God"?
   Ezra, Ezekiel, Micah, Malachi
4) Fill in the blank from 2 Timothy: "All scripture is given by _____ of God."
   Mercy, inspiration, salvation, proof
5) What was the first bird Noah released from the window of the ark (and did not return)?
   A raven, a pigeon, a sparrow, a dove
6) In 2 Kings, what creatures ate the carcass of Jezebel?
   She-bears, dogs, frogs, worms

ANSWERS:
1) Neither. (Edom, another name for Esau, was also a land.)
2) Rahab (Joshua 2:1, 6).
3) Ezekiel (Ezekiel 1:1).
4) Inspiration (2 Timothy 3:16).
5) A raven (Genesis 8:6 – 7).
6) Dogs (2 Kings 9:10).

Score Correct _____ Date_____ Name _____
Study Notes:_____
_____

Quiz 49

1) Is the book of Gedaliah in the Old Testament, the New Testament, or neither?
2) Who worked seven years to earn a wife (Rachel)?
   Isaiah, Abraham, Jacob, Joshua
3) There are four Beatitudes in the book of Luke and how many in the book of Matthew?
   Two, four, six, eight
4) In Joel 3, what was the holy mountain of the Lord?
   Sinai, Zion, Nebo, Moriah
5) What name did the apostles give to Joses?
   Laban, Barnabas, Tiras, Jeezer
6) Who was Timothy's mother?
   Abigail, Miriam, Eunice, Rachel

ANSWERS:
1) Neither. (Gedaliah was a son of Ahikam and grandson of Shaphan.)
2) Jacob (Genesis 29:20 – 21).
3) Eight (Matthew 5:3 – 12).
4) Zion (Joel 3:17).
5) Barnabas (Acts 4:36).
6) Eunice (2 Timothy 1:5).

Score Correct _____ Date _____ Name _____

Study Notes: _____

_____

Quiz 50

1) Is the book of Gethsemane in the Old Testament, the New Testament, or neither?
2) In Genesis 32, who was "greatly afraid and distressed" about a reunion with a brother he had wronged?
   Joseph, Jacob, Aaron, Peter
3) God asked Ezekiel to divide up his _____?
   Land, house, sons, hair
4) Which book begins: "The former treatise have I made, O Theophilus, of all that Jesus began both to do and teach."?
   Matthew, Luke, John, Acts
5) Where did Elkanah live that was one of the towns in the tribal territories of Ephraim?
   Tel Arad, Ramah, Kartan, Yavne
6) Fill in the blank from Galatians, "Stand fast therefore in the _____ wherewith Christ hath made us free."
   Freedom, liberty, choice, spirit

ANSWERS:

1) Neither. (Gethsemane is a garden at the foot of the Mont of Olives in Jerusalem, Israel.)
2) Jacob (Genesis 32:4 – 7).
3) Hair (Ezekiel 5:1).
4) Acts (Acts 1:1).
5) Ramah (1 Samuel 2:11).
6) Liberty (Galatians 5:1).

Score Correct _____ Date _____ Name _____
Study Notes: _____

Quiz 51

1) Is the book of Iscah in the Old Testament, the New Testament, or neither?
2) In 2 Timothy, Paul said he endured persecution for whose sake that they may also obtain salvation?
   Fellow followers, the elect, evil doers, the unwitnessed
3) Which apostle denied he knew Jesus?
   John, Thomas, Judas, Peter
4) The sun stood still while Joshua's army destroyed what people?
   Amorites, Midianites, Egyptians, Philistines
5) Who was David's oldest brother?
   Jonah, Eliab, Joel, Agrippa
6) In Genesis 9, who saw a rainbow in the sky?
   Adam, Moses, Noah, Abraham

ANSWERS:

1) Neither. (Iscah was a daughter of Haran, Abraham's younger brother.)
2) The elect (2 Timothy 2:10).
3) Peter (Matthew 26:69 – 74).
4) Amorites (Joshua 10:6 – 7, 12 – 13).
5) Eliab (1 Samuel 17:13 – 14).
6) Noah (Genesis 9:15 – 17).

Score Correct_____ Date_____ Name _____
Study Notes:_____
_____

Quiz 52

1) Is the book of Abigail in the Old Testament, the New Testament, or neither?

2) In 2 Timothy, which Alexander did much evil to Paul?
Alexander the Great, Alexander of Mesopotamia, Alexander the coppersmith, Alexander of Damascus

3) Fill in the blank from Proverbs: "A man that hath friends must shew himself friendly: and there is a friend that sticketh closer than a _____."?
Mate, brother, sister, faithful pet

4) Who was David's first wife and Saul's youngest daughter?
Michal, Mahalath, Merab, Matred

5) How many children did Hannah have, including Samuel?
Five, ten, fifteen, twenty

6) What did Moses use to afflict boils upon man, beast, and all of Egypt?
Ashes of the furnace, river water, lamb's blood, sour wine

ANSWERS:

1) Neither. (Abigail was a wife of David.)
2) Alexander the coppersmith (2 Timothy 4:14).
3) Brother (Proverbs 18:24).
4) Michal (1 Samuel 18:27 – 28).
5) Five (1 Samuel 2:21).
6) Ashes of the furnace (Exodus 9:8 – 11).

Score Correct_____ Date_____ Name _____
*Study Notes:*_____
_____

Quiz 53

1) Is the book of Lydia in the Old Testament, the New Testament, or neither?
2) How many of the ten plagues of Egypt involved "swarms"?
   Two, four, five, six
3) In Proverbs 15, what does a soft answer turneth away, but grievous words stir up anger?
   Wisdom, scorn, wrath, fear
4) Who begat David, thus was his father?
   Moses, Noah, Abraham, Jesse
5) The eating of "what" in any manner is completely prohibited in Leviticus 17?
   Mud, blood, vines, snow
6) Ephraim, one of the twelve tribes comprising Israel, is described as what animal without heart in Hosea 7?
   Silly dove, talking ass (donkey), running hare, slippery serpent

ANSWERS:
1) Neither. (Lydia was a Christian woman and a seller of purple.)
2) Four (frogs: Exodus 8:3; lice: Exodus 8:16 – 17; flies: Exodus 8:21; locusts: Exodus 10:12 – 13).
3) Wrath (Proverbs 15:1).
4) Jesse (Matthew 1:6; David was youngest of eight sons).
5) Blood (Leviticus 17:10 – 12).
6) Silly dove (Hosea 7:11).

Score Correct_____ Date_____ Name _____
Study Notes:_____

_____

Quiz 54

1) Is the book of Judges in the Old Testament, the New Testament, or neither?

2) In Genesis 27, who was the father blessing his second-born son, Jacob, as he said, "Come near now, and kiss me, my son."?
   Isaac, Iddo, Isaiah, Iscariot

3) How many windows were in Noah's Ark?
   Zero, one, seven, fifty-two

4) Paul says to feed thine enemy if hungry and give him drink if thirsty, as doing so shall heap "what" upon his head?
   Pains of pain, coals of fire, pails of trouble, winds of ice

5) In Proverbs, what are the glory of children?
   Dreams, their fathers, laughter and devotion, sweet past times

6) What town near Gath did Achish give to David?
   Ziklag, Jerusalem, Zoan, Kartan

ANSWERS:

1) Old Testament. (Judges is the seventh book of the Old Testament.)
2) Isaac (Genesis 27:22 – 26).
3) One (Genesis 6:16, 8:6).
4) Coals of fire (Romans 12:20).
5) Their fathers (Proverbs 17:6).
6) Ziklag (1 Samuel 27:5 – 7).

Score Correct _____ Date _____ Name _____
Study Notes: _____
_____

Joseph Sold by His Brothers

Quiz 55

1) Is the book of Laban in the Old Testament, the New Testament, or neither?

2) What was the second bird, after the raven, that Noah released from the window of the ark?
Eagle, pigeon, sparrow, dove

3) In Proverbs, what are as an honeycomb, sweet to the soul, and health to the bones?
Children smiling, pleasant words, joyful noises, willing givers

4) In Judges 1, who fed seventy kings at his table?
Benaiah, Nebuchadnezzar, Adonibezek, Mephibosheth

5) To deter the transport, passage, and sale of goods on the Sabbath in Jerusalem, what did Nehemiah command?
Heavy taxation, impounding of carts, gates should be shut, peddlers be stoned

6) The days of Purim were named for Pur, which means what?
The pure in heart, the lot, the pagans, the poverty

ANSWERS:

1) Neither. (Laban was the brother of Rebekah and father of Rachel and Leah.)

2) Dove (Genesis 8:6 – 8).

3) Pleasant words (Proverbs 16:24).

4) Adonibezek (Judges 1:7).

5) Gates should be shut (Nehemiah 13:15 – 19).

6) The lot (Esther 9:24 – 26).

Score Correct_____ Date_____ Name _____

Study Notes:_____

Quiz 56

1) Is the book of Naomi in the Old Testament, the New Testament, or neither?
2) Which of this group was not on the Mount of Transfiguration with Jesus?
   Peter, James, John, Andrew
3) What Egyptian name did Pharaoh call Joseph in the book of Genesis?
   Zaphnathpaaneah, Merodach-Baladan, Meraioth, Zalmunna
4) From Proverbs, what goeth before destruction, and an haughty spirit before a fall?
   Deceit, adultery, anger, pride
5) Who loved many strange women and had three hundred concubines?
   Pharaoh, King Solomon, Saul, Herod
6) In which city did king Ahasuerus live?
   Corinth, Gath, Berea, Shushan

ANSWERS:

1) Neither. (Naomi was married to Elimelech and the mother-in-law of Ruth.)
2) Andrew (Matthew 17:1 – 2).
3) Zaphnathpaaneah (Genesis 41:45).
4) Pride (Proverbs 16:18).
5) King Solomon (1 Kings 11:1 – 3).
6) Shushan (Esther 1:2).

Score Correct _____ Date _____ Name _____

Study Notes: _____

_____

Quiz 57

1) Is the book of Othniel in the Old Testament, the New Testament, or neither?
2) Who was the wife of Joseph?
   Tamar, Rebekah, Asenath, Taphanes
3) Fill in the blank from Proverbs: "The way of the _____ is an abomination unto the Lord: but he loveth him that followeth after righteousness."
   Wicked, unjust, lazy, hypocrites
4) At God's instruction Noah sealed the ark inside and out with what to make it watertight?
   Pitch, animal soap, borage, cedar sap
5) When the Lord established his covenant with Abram, what did he change Abram's name to?
   Simon Peter, Aaron, Moses, Abraham
6) Jehu instructed whom to be thrown down from a window to be trampled by his horses?
   Ahab, Jezebel, Delilah, Antiochus

ANSWERS:
1) Neither. (Othniel was Caleb's younger brother and a judge in Israel for forty years.)
2) Asenath (Genesis 41:45).
3) Wicked (Proverbs 15:9).
4) Pitch (Genesis 6:13 – 14).
5) Abraham (Genesis 17:4 – 5).
6) Jezebel (2 Kings 9:30 – 33).

Score Correct_____ Date_____ Name _____
*Study Notes:*_____
_____

Quiz 58

1) Is the book of Philemon in the Old Testament, the New Testament, or neither?

2) To whom was the Lord speaking to when he said, "Take me an heifer of three years old, and a she goat of three years old, and a ram of three years old, and a turtledove, and a young pigeon."?
Judas, Paul, Abram, Isaac

3) In Genesis 4, who is considered the father of all musicians?
Jeremiah, Joash, Jubal, Job

4) Which book begins, "Then Moab rebelled against Israel after the death of Ahab."?
Exodus, 2 Kings, Job, Proverbs

5) From Luke 7, in what town did Jesus raise a widow's son from the dead?
Ashdod, Nain, Golan, Tanis

6) As noted in Acts 24, Felix's wife Drusilla was a _____?
Pharisee, Gentile, Greek, Jewess

ANSWERS:

1) New Testament. (Philemon is the eighteenth book of the New Testament.)

2) Abram (Genesis 15:3 – 9).

3) Jubal (Genesis 4:21).

4) 2 Kings (2 Kings 1:1).

5) Nain (Luke 7:11 – 15).

6) Jewess (Acts 24:24).

Score Correct_____ Date_____ Name _____
Study Notes:_____
_____

Quiz 59

1) Is the book of 1 Peter in the Old Testament, the New Testament, or neither?

2) Where did Peter cure Aeneas, who had been bedridden for eight years and was sick of the palsy?
Tyre, Neapolis, Lydda, Gibeon

3) According to 2 Timothy, what wicked contemporaries resisted Moses?
Nahash/Doeg, Esau/Korah, Jannes/Jambres, Antipas/Cain

4) Which book begins, "The former treatise have I made, O Theophilus, of all that Jesus began both to do and teach."?
Matthew, Luke, John, Acts

5) Where did Aaron the priest die?
Mount of Olives, Pisgah, Mount Hor, Gilboa

6) In 2 Kings, what Philistine city worshipped Baalzebub?
Ekron, Succoth, Gomorrah, Antipatris

ANSWERS:

1) New Testament. (1 Peter is the twenty-first book of the New Testament.)
2) Lydda (Acts 9:32 – 34).
3) Jannes/Jambres (2 Timothy 3:8).
4) Acts (Acts 1:1).
5) Mount Hor (Numbers 33:38).
6) Ekron (2 Kings 1:3).

Score Correct_____ Date_____ Name _____
Study Notes:_____
_____

Quiz 60

1) Is the book of Philesians in the Old Testament, the New Testament, or neither?

2) What were Gihon, Pison, Hiddekel, and Euphrates, as connected with the Garden of Eden?
   Serpents, kings, rivers, caves

3) In Revelation, what city was said by author John to have "Satan's seat"?
   Pergamos, Miletus, Patara, Sodom

4) Who was the son of Jehoiada who killed an Egyptian giant, five cubits (seven-and-a-half feet) high?
   Benaiah, Gideon, Jannes, Baruch

5) In 1 Kings, who is given credit for writing a thousand and five songs?
   Jacob, Solomon, Philip, David

6) Who carried a letter from the king of Syria to the king of Israel?
   Stephen, Naaman, John the Baptist, Delilah

ANSWERS:

1) Neither. (Philesians is fictitious combination of Philippians and Ephesians of the New Testament.)

2) Rivers (Genesis 2:8 – 15).

3) Pergamos (Revelation 2:12 – 13).

4) Benaiah (1 Chronicles 11:22 – 23).

5) Solomon (1 Kings 4:30 – 32).

6) Naaman (2 Kings 5:1 – 6).

Score Correct _____ Date _____ Name _____
Study Notes: _____

_____

Quiz 61

1) Is the book of Stephen in the Old Testament, the New Testament, or neither?

2) Where did Jacob have his famous dream of a ladder resting on the earth, with its top reaching to heaven, and the angels of God ascending and descending on it?
Lachish, Perga, Haran, Bethel

3) What was blown out of Egypt by a mighty strong west wind and cast into the Red Sea?
Unclean spirits, locusts, sinners, night

4) Adam and Eve had how many total children?
Two sons, two sons and two daughters, three sons, many sons and daughters

5) Who made an axe head float after it had broken off and fallen into the river Jordan?
Elisha, Apelles, Jamlech, Paruah

6) When the Lord returns, those who are saved will meet him where?
Armageddon fields, in the air, Jerusalem, Mount Sinai

ANSWERS:

1) Neither. (Stephen was the first martyr of the Christian Church, being stoned to death.)

2) Bethel (Genesis 28:12, 19).

3) Locusts (Exodus 10:19).

4) Many sons and daughters (Genesis 5:4).

5) Elisha (2 Kings 6:2 – 6).

6) In the air (1 Thessalonians 4:15 – 17).

Score Correct_____ Date_____ Name _____

Study Notes:_____

Quiz 62

1) Is the book of Adonijah in the Old Testament, the New Testament, or neither?

2) Whose job was to lay next to the aging king David and keep him warm?
Basemeth, Shelomit, Zillah, Abishag

3) Which book's first chapter begins, "God, who at sundry times and in divers manners spake in time past unto the fathers by the prophets."?
Mark, Galatians, Hebrews, Jude

4) Moses smote the rock at Horeb because his people needed what?
Food, God's gesture, water, shelter

5) Who was the friend and personal advisor of Abimelech, a king of Gerar?
Adalia, Ahuzzath, Agag, Aharhel

6) Whose last words were, "What is there done, my son"?
Samson, John, Eli, Paul

ANSWERS:
1) Neither. (Adonijah was the fourth son of David and Haggith.)
2) Abishag (1 Kings 1:1 – 3).
3) Hebrews (Hebrews 1:1).
4) Water (Exodus 17:5 – 6).
5) Ahuzzath (Genesis 26:26).
6) Eli (1 Samuel 4:15 – 18).

Score Correct _____ Date _____ Name _____

Study Notes: _____

_____

Quiz 63

1) Is the book of Cyrus in the Old Testament, the New Testament, or neither?
2) God forbids the intermarriage of near kin by stating thou shalt not uncover their _____?
   Beliefs, nakedness, garments, lusts
3) Fill in the blank from the book of Romans: "Neither death, life, angels, principalities, powers, things present, nor things to come, shall be able to separate us from the _____ of God."
   Depths, vengeance, wisdom, love
4) What can no man serve two of, for he will hate the one and love the other?
   Mates, masters, warlords, occupations
5) Who did Jacob kiss the first time he saw her (later becoming her husband) during the watering of sheep?
   Ahlai, Rachel, Iscah, Jemima
6) What mountain provided the setting of the burning bush during Moses' encounter with God?
   Horeb, Pisgah, Sinai, Zion

ANSWERS:

1) Neither. (Cyrus was the founder of the Persian Empire.)
2) Nakedness (Leviticus 18:6 – 18).
3) Love (Romans 8:38 – 39).
4) Masters (Matthew 6:24).
5) Rachel (Genesis 29:9 – 11).
6) Horeb (Exodus 3:1 – 2).

Score Correct _____ Date _____ Name _____
Study Notes: _____

_____

Quiz 64

1) Is the book of Candace in the Old Testament, the New Testament, or neither?
2) Who begat Nimrod, a "mighty hunter" before the Lord?
   Besodeiah, Cush, Dathan, Peresh
3) Before his anointing as king, what job did the young David have?
   Cupbearer, shepherd, farmer, tentmaker
4) What word did Jesus pair with "Alpha" referring to himself as the beginning and the end, the first and the last?
   Final, Termination, Omega, Harvest
5) Who asked Jesus, "What is truth?" and afterwards saith, "I find in him no fault at all."?
   Herod, Pilate, John the Baptist, Caiaphas
6) In Judges 14, what man offered thirty changes of garments for solving a riddle?
   Moses, Samson, Peter, Solomon

ANSWERS:
1) Neither. (Candace was an Ethiopian queen.)
2) Cush (Genesis 10:8 – 9).
3) Shepherd (1 Samuel 16:11 – 13).
4) Omega (Revelation 22:13).
5) Pilate (John 18:38).
6) Samson (Judges 14:12).

Score Correct _____ Date_____ Name _____
Study Notes: _____
_____

Quiz 65

1) Is the book of Amos in the Old Testament, the New Testament, or neither?
2) Fill in the blank from Psalm 118: "It is better to trust in the Lord than to put _____ in man."
   Finances, confidence, hope, harvests
3) What heavenly sound accompanied God's work at Pentecost?
   A mighty wind, a wolf howling, trumpets blowing, a multitude cheers
4) Where is the Apostles' Creed found in the Bible?
   Nowhere, Matthew 3, James 5, Revelation 11
5) The word "catholic" means universal as in the universal church, and is specifically found in how many verses of the Bible?
   Zero, 16, 42, 178
6) What does the book of Job describe as the "king of terrors"?
   Loneliness without God, hunger, crops failing, death

ANSWERS:

1) Old Testament. (Amos is the thirtieth book of the Old Testament.)
2) Confidence (Psalm 118:8).
3) A mighty wind (Acts 2:1 – 2).
4) Nowhere. (It was devised at least 150 years later as a record of what the apostles taught.)
5) Zero. (The word originally applied to all Christians as members of the Body of Christ.)
6) Death (Job 18:13 – 14).

Score Correct_____ Date_____ Name _____

*Study Notes:*_____

_____

Quiz 66

1) Is the book of Belial in the Old Testament, the New Testament, or neither?

2) Where is the phrase "communion of the saints" found in the Bible, as it refers to believers in the past, present, and future sharing a common salvation?
   Matthew 6:12, Romans 7:1, Revelation 22:18, it's not

3) What did Jesus promise the Heavenly Father would give to anyone who asked?
   Bread of life, food and drink, Holy Spirit, eternal life

4) In Revelation 15, what musical instrument accompanies the song of victorious saints over the beast?
   Drums, harps, timbrels, trumpets

5) At the end of times, what will be so scarce that seven women will seek after each one?
   Homes, men, loaves of bread, children

6) Whose wife advised her husband, "Curse God, and die."?
   David, Job, Joseph, Pharaoh

ANSWERS:

1) Neither. (Belial came to be known as a proper name for the Devil or Satan in the New Testament.)

2) It's not. (It is an important part of the Apostles' Creed.)

3) Holy Spirit (Luke 11:13).

4) Harps (Revelation 15:1 – 4).

5) Men (Isaiah 4:1).

6) Job (Job 2:9).

Score Correct _____ Date _____ Name _____

Study Notes: _____

_____

Quiz 67

1) Is the book of Capernaum in the Old Testament, the New Testament, or neither?

2) Isaiah uses a parable that compares a vineyard to the _____?
   House of Israel, darkness, wrath of God, saints

3) Colossians says we should set our affection on things above, not on things on the _____?
   Guess, heart, earth, shadows

4) Which book says that blind, or broken, or maimed animals must not be sacrificed unto the Lord?
   Exodus, Leviticus, Numbers, Deuteronomy

5) In Acts 20, who was taken up as dead after falling from the third loft during Paul's long preaching?
   Eutychus, Forunatus, Gabbai, Naasson

6) Upon what "mountains of" became the final stopping point for Noah's ark?
   Hermon, Gerizim, Ararat, Lebanon

ANSWERS:

1) Neither. (Capernaum was a small fishing village on the northern shore of the Sea of Galilee.)

2) House of Israel (Isaiah 5:7).

3) Earth (Colossians 3:1 – 2).

4) Leviticus (Leviticus 22:22).

5) Eutychus (Acts 20:9 – 10).

6) Ararat (Genesis 8:4).

Score Correct _____ Date_____ Name _____
Study Notes:_____

Quiz 68

1) Is the book of Wormwood in the Old Testament, the New Testament, or neither?
2) Fill in the blank from Proverbs: "He that spareth his rod _____ his son."
   Loveth, spoileth, asketh, hateth
3) In the book of Hosea, who found Israel like grapes in the wilderness?
   Phicol, the Lord, Samiah, Zelophehad
4) After Jesus blessed the disciples' efforts, how many fish did Simon Peter catch?
   None, 4, 153, a net full
5) King Asa in the thirty and ninth year of his reign was inflicted with a disease in what part of his body?
   Neck, stomach, arms, feet
6) What color are the seven candlesticks in Revelation?
   Black, white, silver, golden

ANSWERS:

1) Neither. (Wormwood is mentioned in eight verses, usually with the implication of bitterness.)
2) Hateth (Proverbs 13:24).
3) The Lord (Hosea 9:10).
4) 153 (John 21:10 – 11).
5) Feet (2 Chronicles 16:12).
6) Golden (Revelation 1:20).

Score Correct _____ Date_____ Name _____
Study Notes: _____
_____

Quiz 69

1) Is the book of Zimri in the Old Testament, the New Testament, or neither?

2) To which apostle did Christ commit the care of his mother while he was dying on the cross?
   James, John, Peter, Jude

3) In the book of Matthew, how is the name "Emmanuel" interpreted?
   Holy One, God with us, friend of man, Heavenly Father

4) How many are better than one because they have a good reward for their labour?
   Two, three, five, seven

5) To whom did God give a bill of divorce?
   Adam and Eve, Egypt, Boaz and Ruth, Israel

6) The verse of Daniel 4:37 contains every letter of the alphabet except?
   C, q, w, x

ANSWERS:

1) Neither. (Zimri was the son of Salu and slain by Phinehas.)
2) John (John 19:26 – 27).
3) God with us (Matthew 1:23).
4) Two (Ecclesiastes 4:9).
5) Israel (Jeremiah 3:8).
6) Q (Now I Nebuchadnezzar praise and extol and honour the King of heaven, all whose works are truth, and his ways judgment: and those that walk in pride he is able to abase).

Score Correct _____ Date _____ Name _____
Study Notes: _____

_____

Quiz 70

1) Is the book of Uzziah in the Old Testament, the New Testament, or neither?

2) After the multitude of about five thousand ate their fill of the five loaves and two fishes, how many baskets of food were left over?
None, two, five, twelve

3) Who did the Lord describe to Satan as "a perfect and an upright man, one that feareth God, and escheweth evil."?
Son of God, Job, John the Baptist, Noah

4) What "Mount" was famous as the source of timber for Solomon's Temple?
Tabor, Nebo, Lebanon, Seir

5) How did Judas identify Jesus on betraying him to the soldiers?
Seized his hand, kissed him, embraced him, passed him bread

6) What were the two animals that spoke to humans in Genesis and Numbers?
Horse and camel, ram and cow, serpent and ass (donkey), dog and eagle

ANSWERS:

1) Neither. (Uzziah was a good king of Judah.)
2) Twelve (Matthew 14:19 – 21).
3) Job (Job 1: 7 – 8).
4) Lebanon (1 Kings 5:2 – 6).
5) Gave him a kiss (Matthew 26:47 – 49).
6) Serpent and ass (donkey) (Genesis 3:1 – 4; Numbers 22:28 – 30).

Score Correct _____ Date _____ Name _____

Study Notes: _____

_____

Quiz 71

1) Is the book of Acts in the Old Testament, the New Testament, or neither?

2) How many of Job's friends came to his comfort, after Satan smote him with sore boils?
   Zero, one, two, three

3) Who restored Saul's sight in Damascus by putting his hands on him that he be filled with the Holy Ghost?
   Aeneas, Alphaeus, Ananias, Aniezer

4) As mentioned only once in the Bible, who was the Eznite that was one of David's heroes who lifted up his spear against eight hundred?
   Adino, Hur, Irad, Seba

5) How many levels of decks or stories were in Noah's ark?
   One, two, three, four

6) What was Jesus' final word spoken as recorded in the book of Revelation?
   Justly, quickly, reverently, lovingly

ANSWERS:

1) New Testament. (Acts is the fifth book of the New Testament.)
2) Three (Job 2:7 – 11).
3) Ananias (Acts 9:17 – 19).
4) Adino (2 Samuel 23:8).
5) Three (Genesis 6:16).
6) Quickly (Revelation 22:20).

Score Correct _____ Date _____ Name _____
Study Notes: _____
_____

Quiz 72

1) Is the book of Deborah in the Old Testament, the New Testament, or neither?

2) How many devils came out of Mary called Magdalene when she was healed of evil spirits?
   One, three, five, seven

3) Two bodies of water were parted in the Bible; one was the Red Sea, and what was the other, which had been parted on two separate occasions?
   Gihon River, Sea of Galilee, Mediterranean Sea, Jordan River

4) In the book of Romans, how does faith come about?
   Hearing the word of God, worshipping, making of joyful noises, praying

5) What was the name of the high priest's servant, who had his ear cut off by Simon Peter when he attempted to protect Jesus from being taken as a prisoner?
   Ahira, Galus, Malchus, Titus

6) Who was Hananiah's father?
   Abiah, Azur, Allon, Aretas

ANSWERS:

1) Neither. (Deborah was the only female judge mentioned in the Bible.)

2) Seven (Luke 8:2).

3) Jordan River (Joshua 3:15 – 17, 2 Kings 2:6 – 8).

4) Hearing the word of God (Romans 10:17).

5) Malchus (John 18:10).

6) Azur (Jeremiah 28:1).

Score Correct _____ Date _____ Name _____

Study Notes: _____

_____

Balaam and the Talking Donkey

Quiz 73

1) Is the book of Galilee in the Old Testament, the New Testament, or neither?

2) At approximately a height of ten feet, Goliath was how many cubits and a span tall?
Four, six, eight, ten

3) Among its different names, the Sea of Galilee was also called the Lake of _____?
Merom, Gennesaret, Ebal, Horeb

4) In the book of Romans, man is justified by what?
Faith, loving one another, deeds, rejoicing

5) How many sons did Gideon begat?
None, seven, twelve and one, threescore and ten

6) In the Book of Luke, what is the city of David called?
Nazareth, Dothan, Beersheba, Bethlehem

ANSWERS:

1) Neither. (The Sea of Galilee is Israel's largest freshwater lake.)

2) Six (1 Samuel 17:4).

3) Gennesaret (Luke 5:1).

4) Faith (Romans 3:27 – 28).

5) Threescore and ten (Judges 8:30).

6) Bethlehem (Luke 2:4).

Score Correct _____ Date_____ Name _____
Study Notes: _____
_____

Quiz 74

1) Is the book of Laodicea in the Old Testament, the New Testament, or neither?
2) What menacing creatures came in droves and bit much of the people of Israel in the wilderness, causing deaths?
   Stinging locusts, fiery serpents, loathing dogs, screaming demons
3) Who asked God, "Shall not the Judge of all the earth do right"?
   Hattil, Abraham, Imrah, Rabmag
4) In 1 Kings 4, how many officers (governors) did king Solomon have over all Israel?
   12, 61, 100, 192
5) What relationship were Ishmael and Isaac?
   None, father and son, cousins, half brothers
6) Who was Abraham's wife after Sarai (Sarah)?
   Antiochus, Jerusha, Baara, Keturah

ANSWERS:

1) Neither. (Laodicea, the city mentioned in the Bible, lay on the confines of Phrygia and Lydia.)
2) Fiery serpents (Numbers 21:5 – 6).
3) Abraham (Genesis 18:23 – 25).
4) 12 (1 Kings 4:7).
5) Half brothers (Genesis 16:15, 21:3).
6) Keturah (Genesis 17:15, 25:1).

Score Correct_____ Date_____ Name _____
Study Notes:_____
_____

Quiz 75

1) Is the book of 2 Peter in the Old Testament, the New Testament, or neither?

2) In Acts 16, what city was the home of Lydia, a seller of purple?
   Derbe, Thyatira, Samaria, Jericho

3) Who said, "The Lord is my rock, and my fortress, and my deliverer."?
   David, Samuel, Peter, Solomon

4) "The book of the generation of Jesus Christ, the son of David, the son of Abraham" is the first verse of which book?
   Matthew, Mark, Luke, John

5) Which of Jacob's wives or concubines was first to bear a child (a son named Reuben)?
   Leah, Rachel, Bilhah, Zilpah

6) In Acts 22, what famous rabbi was Paul's teacher?
   Hillel, Turkel, Zakkai, Gamaliel

ANSWERS:

1) New Testament. (2 Peter is the twenty-second book of the New Testament.)

2) Thyatira (Acts 16:14).

3) David (2 Samuel 22:1 – 2).

4) Matthew (Matthew 1:1).

5) Leah (Genesis 29:28 – 32).

6) Gamaliel (Acts 22:3).

Score Correct _____ Date _____ Name _____

Study Notes: _____

_____

Quiz 76

1) Is the book of Nicodemus in the Old Testament, the New Testament, or neither?

2) Who was clothed in the wilderness with his raiment of camel's hair and a leathern girdle about his loins?
John the Baptist, Jesus, Ozias, Abdeel

3) What city was home to Mary, Martha, and Lazarus?
Corinth, Gaza, Bethany, Sardis

4) According to Paul in the book of Romans, how many righteous people are there?
None, fifty, seven thousand, all who are pure in heart

5) Noah was somewhere between how many years of age (as the Bible does not specify) when he started building the ark?
100 – 200, 300 – 400, 500 – 600, 700 – 800

6) What was the relationship of Abram to Lot?
Father, brother, uncle, grandfather

ANSWERS:

1) Neither. (Nicodemus was a man of the Pharisees.)
2) John the Baptist (Matthew 3:1 – 4).
3) Bethany (John 11:1).
4) None (Romans 3:10).
5) 500 – 600 (Genesis 5:32).
6) Uncle (Genesis 11:27).

Score Correct _____ Date _____ Name _____

Study Notes: _____

_____

Quiz 77

1) Is the book of 3 Thessalonians in the Old Testament, the New Testament, or neither?
2) What was the vale of Siddim, an area of Sodom and Gomorrah, also referred to as?
   Sicketh friend, salt sea, great plain, naked truth
3) How many times is the word "Bible" mentioned in the scripture of the Bible?
   Zero, three, forty-nine, over one thousand
4) Which of these was not a son of Noah?
   Shem, Ham, Levi, Japheth
5) In Matthew 13, what baking item did Jesus compare to the kingdom of heaven?
   Eggs, milk, salt, yeast
6) Which of these was celebrated for its medicinal qualities?
   Mamre, balm, linen, perez

ANSWERS:

1) Neither. (3 Thessalonians is fictitious, but 1 and 2 Thessalonians are the thirteenth and fourteenth books of the New Testament.)
2) Salt sea (Genesis 14:3).
3) Zero. (The word "Bible" is not present in any verses.)
4) Levi (Genesis 6:10).
5) Yeast (Matthew 13:33).
6) Balm (Jeremiah 46:11, 51:8).

Score Correct_____ Date_____ Name _____
Study Notes: _____
_____

Quiz 78

1) Is the book of Rhoda in the Old Testament, the New Testament, or neither?

2) To whom did Jesus say, "Man shall not live by bread alone, but by every word that proceedeth out of the mouth of God."?
The devil, Judas Iscariot, Mary Magdalene, John the Baptist

3) Moses was so-named because he was drawn out of the _____?
Mountain, water, skies, fields

4) Who was the son of Elmodam and an ancestor of Jesus, mentioned only once in the Bible?
Cosam, Necho, Vajezatha, Zabud

5) What river (though not specifically mentioned by name) was turned into blood by Moses, as a sign from God?
Pison, Nile, Euphrates, Gihon

6) Who founded the city of Enoch, so named for his son?
Cyrenius, Cain, Blastus, Abialbon

ANSWERS:

1) Neither. (Rhoda was a maiden damsel living in the house of Mary.)

2) The devil (Matthew 4:1 – 4).

3) Water (Exodus 2:9 – 10).

4) Cosam (Luke 3:23 – 24, 28).

5) Nile (Exodus 7:17 – 25).

6) Cain (Genesis 4:17).

Score Correct_____ Date_____ Name _____
Study Notes:_____
_____

Quiz 79

1) Is the book of Tiberius in the Old Testament, the New Testament, or neither?

2) Who was the disciple that was the unsuccessful candidate for apostleship to replace Judas, losing out to Matthias?
Justus, Porcius, Julius, Kishi

3) How many days had Lazarus been dead before being risen by Jesus?
Two, three, four, seven

4) What "people of" put on sackcloth to show their repentance before God?
Israel, Judah, Nineveh, Mordecai

5) On the night of the Lord's Passover to execute judgment, who was to die in Egyptian households?
Concubines, the firstborn, the eldest, the unsaved

6) In Song of Solomon, what cannot quench love?
False hearts, many waters, friends, death

ANSWERS:

1) Neither. (Tiberius Caesar Augustus was the third emperor of Rome and also the name of a city on the Sea of Galilee.)

2) Justus (a surname of Joseph of Barsabas; Acts 1:23 – 26).

3) Four (John 11:39 – 43).

4) Nineveh (Jonah 3:5).

5) The firstborn (Exodus 12:11 – 12).

6) Many waters (Song of Solomon 8:7).

Score Correct _____ Date _____ Name _____

Study Notes: _____

_____

Quiz 80

1) Is the book of Sarepta in the Old Testament, the New Testament, or neither?
2) Which Gospel speaks of Pilate writing a title, The King of the Jews, on a notice fastened on Jesus' cross?
   Matthew, Mark, Luke, John
3) Which day of creation included God making the darkness he called night?
   First, second, fourth, sixth
4) What form did the Spirit of God take when it descended on Jesus after his baptism by John the Baptist?
   Gentle wind, hare, thunderous roar, dove
5) In Exodus, which was the last plague of the ten on?
   Water into blood, death of the firstborn, fiery hail, locusts
6) What did Paul say should be "seasoned with salt"?
   Your speech, unclean animals, fishes of the river, one's enemies

ANSWERS:
1) Neither. (Sarepta was a city of Sidon on the Mediterranean coast.)
2) John (John 19:19 – 21).
3) First (Genesis 1:5).
4) Dove (Matthew 3:13 – 16).
5) Death of the firstborn (Exodus chapters 7 – 12, with the final plague listed in 12:29).
6) Your speech (Colossians 4:6, 18).

Score Correct_____ Date_____ Name _____
Study Notes:_____
_____

Quiz 81

1) Is the book of Ecclesiastes in the Old Testament, the New Testament, or neither?
2) Fill in the blank from Psalm 119: "Thy word is a _____ unto my feet, and a light unto my path."
   Bath, comfort, covering, lamp
3) Where was king David buried so that he slept with his fathers?
   Netophah, Bethharam, Shaaraim, the city of David
4) In the book of Revelation, how many pearly gates are there to the new Jerusalem?
   One, seven, twelve, twenty
5) What does a proverb say is strongest among beasts?
   Elephant, lion, camel, the devil
6) Who was the king of Assyria that invaded Israel in the days of Menahem and was bribed to turn back?
   Raddai, Pul, Zippor, Abiasaph

ANSWERS:

1) Old Testament. (Ecclesiastes is the twenty-first book of the Old Testament.)
2) Lamp (Psalm 119:105).
3) The city of David (which was Old Jerusalem; 1 Kings 2:10).
4) Twelve (Revelation 21:2, 21).
5) Lion (Proverbs 30:30).
6) Pul (2 Kings 15:19 – 20).

Score Correct_____ Date_____ Name _____
Study Notes:_____

_____

Quiz 82

1) Is the book of Eli in the Old Testament, the New Testament, or neither?

2) Whose flock was Moses attending when the Lord appeared to him in a flame out of the midst of a bush?
Jethro, his own, Aaron, Shalmaneser

3) Which was not one of Goliath's chosen arms for fighting with David?
Sword, spear, bow and arrow, shield

4) What was the name of the brass serpent Moses had made which the children of Israel had worshipped by burning incense to it?
Dagon, Tartak, Nehushtan, Kalwan

5) Which king served as judge saying to bring him a sword to divide the living child in two, when two harlots were fighting over a child?
Menaham, Solomon, David, Pekahiah

6) What church was home to a fornicating woman named Jezebel who committed immoral acts?
Zion, Thyatira, New Jerusalem, Antioch

ANSWERS:

1) Neither. (Eli was a high priest and judge of Israel of the family of Ithamar.)
2) Jethro (his father-in-law; Exodus 3:1 – 2).
3) Bow and arrow (1 Samuel 17:45).
4) Nehushtan (2 Kings 18:4).
5) Solomon (1 Kings 3:16, 24 – 25).
6) Thyatira (Revelation 2:18 – 21).

Score Correct_____ Date_____ Name _____

Study Notes: _____

_____

Quiz 83

1) Is the book of Hamath in the Old Testament, the New Testament, or neither?

2) To keep Adam and Eve away after the Fall, what did God place around the tree of life?
Smoking pits, deep moat, cherubims and a flaming sword, walking vipers

3) In the book of Micah, where does God place forgiven sins?
Depths of the sea, heathen hearts, past the stars, fiery pits

4) How old was Abram when Hagar, his mistress, bore him his eldest son, Ishmael?
60, 86, 98, 125

5) In two separate Psalms, David said, "Moab is my _____."
Terrier, washpot, courier, warrior

6) What type water did Jesus offer the Samaritan woman at the well?
Fresh, cool, living, clean

ANSWERS:

1) Neither. (Hamath was the principal city of upper Syria, now called Hama.)

2) Cherubims and a flaming sword (Genesis 3:22 – 24).

3) Depths of the sea (Micah 7:19).

4) 86 (Genesis 16:15 – 16).

5) Washpot (Psalms 60:8 and 108:9).

6) Living (referring to eternal life; John 4:9 – 10).

Score Correct _____ Date _____ Name _____

Study Notes: _____

_____

Quiz 84

1) Is the book of Elisabeth in the Old Testament, the New Testament, or neither?

2) After Jesus healed a man sick of the palsy, what did the man pick up and carry home?
Brother, bed, mother, cart

3) What is the largest number phrase specifically mentioned in the Bible?
Scores upon scores, one hundred thousand, a thousand thousand, thousands of millions

4) In Psalm 5, the throat of enemies is like what?
A siren call, a well of lies, an open sepulchre, a field of white

5) What was the home city of Peter, Andrew, and Philip?
Jeshanah, Arwad, Netophah, Bethsaida

6) Which book begins: "And the Lord spake unto Moses in the wilderness of Sinai"?
Exodus, Leviticus, Numbers, Deuteronomy

ANSWERS:

1) Neither. (Elisabeth was the wife of Zacharias and mother of John the Baptist.)

2) Bed (Matthew 9:2 – 6).

3) Thousands of millions (Genesis 24:60).

4) An open sepulchre (Psalm 5:8 – 9).

5) Bethsaida (John 1:44).

6) Numbers (Numbers 1:1).

Score Correct _____ Date _____ Name _____

Study Notes: _____

_____

Quiz 85

1) Is the book of Agabus in the Old Testament, the New Testament, or neither?
2) Bashan was called the land of _____?
   Milk and honey, Nod, dry bones, giants
3) Who saw three men and the form of the fourth like the Son of God walking in the fiery furnace?
   Solomon, Job, Daniel, Nebuchadnezzar
4) In 1 Corinthians, the Jews require a sign, and the Greeks seek after _____?
   Champions, food, wisdom, love
5) How old was Abraham when he died?
   75, 175, 202, 256
6) In 2 Samuel, who was called Jedidiah through Nathan the prophet?
   David, Amos, Solomon, Joab

ANSWERS:
1) Neither. (Agabus was a Christian prophet in Jerusalem.)
2) Giants (Deuteronomy 3:13).
3) Nebuchadnezzar (Daniel 3:23 – 26).
4) Wisdom (1 Corinthians 1:22).
5) 175 (Genesis 25:7).
6) Solomon (2 Samuel 12:24 – 25).

Score Correct_____ Date_____ Name _____

Study Notes:_____

_____

Quiz 86

1) Is the book of Claudius in the Old Testament, the New Testament, or neither?

2) What prophet ordered the king of Israel to shoot arrows out of a window?
   Paul, Hosea, Elisha, David

3) How many books of the Bible are only three letters long?
   Zero, one, two, three

4) What prophet saw "the tents of Cushan in affliction: and the curtains of the land of Midian did tremble."?
   Japheth, Noah, Hezekiah, Habakkuk

5) Who said unto the Lord, "Increase our faith"?
   Jonah, apostles, Moses, Jacob

6) Who was Timothy's devout grandmother?
   Dorcas, Lydia, Lois, Hannah

ANSWERS:

1) Neither. (Claudius Caesar was the successor of Caligula as Roman emperor.)
2) Elisha (2 Kings 13:15 – 17).
3) One (Job).
4) Habakkuk (Habakkuk 3:7).
5) Apostles (Luke 17:5).
6) Lois (2 Timothy 1:5).

Score Correct _____ Date _____ Name _____

Study Notes: _____

_____

Quiz 87

1) Is the book of Barsabas in the Old Testament, the New Testament, or neither?

2) Among its different names the Sea of Galilee was also called the Sea of _____ and the Sea of _____?
Abarim/Gilboa, Olivet/Tabor, Chinneroth/Tiberias, Bashan/Gilead

3) Who met three men (angels) at a tent door in the plains of Mamre?
Bartholomew, Abraham, Thomas, Simon

4) In Jacob's dream about Bethel, what was the city first called?
Abana, Dor, Hazor, Luz

5) Whose knees "knocked" in terror after seeing the handwriting on the wall?
Belshazzar, Deuel, Lebbaeus, Sheresh

6) In Jesus' Sermon on the Mount regarding prayer, "Ask, and it shall be given you, seek, and ye shall find, knock, and it shall be _____ unto you."
Rendered, returned, sent, opened

ANSWERS:

1) Neither. (Barsabas was the surname of the Joseph nominated with Matthias to succeed Judas as an apostle.)

2) Chinneroth/Tiberias (Joshua 12:3, John 6:1).

3) Abraham (Genesis 18:1 – 2, 6).

4) Luz (Genesis 28:10, 12, 16, 19).

5) Belshazzar (Daniel 5:6 – 9).

6) Opened (Matthew 7:7).

Score Correct _____ Date _____ Name _____

Study Notes: _____

_____

Quiz 88

1) Is the book of 2 Chronicles in the Old Testament, the New Testament, or neither?
2) Jesus said, "For whosoever shall do the will of my Father which is in heaven, the same is my brother, and sister, and ____."
   Friend, kindred, son, mother
3) What was the name of the god of the men of Hamath?
   Ashima, Succothbenoth, Nergal, Adrammelech
4) How many books of the Bible begin with the letter "E" when spelled?
   Zero, two, five, six
5) When Hezekiah learned that Sennacherib had invaded Judah, what did he order his men to do to the water supply?
   Poison it, reroute it, drown sheep and cattle in it, block it
6) What wicked man was captured by the Assyrians but released when God heard his prayers?
   Korah, Manasseh, Amenhotep, Heriodias

ANSWERS:
1) Old Testament. (2 Chronicles is the fourteenth book of the Old Testament.)
2) Mother (Matthew 12:50).
3) Ashima (2 Kings 17:29 – 30).
4) Six (Ecclesiastes, Ephesians, Esther, Exodus, Ezekiel, Ezra).
5) Block it (2 Chronicles 32:1 – 4).
6) Manasseh (2 Chronicles 33:1 – 2, 6, 11 – 13).

Score Correct_____ Date_____ Name _____
Study Notes:_____
_____

Quiz 89

1) Is the book of Hannah in the Old Testament, the New Testament, or neither?

2) Who said on answering the Lord, "The serpent beguiled me, and I did eat."?
Adam, Eve, Cain, Abel

3) What phenomenon had led the wise men to the young Jesus and savior?
Whirlwind, star, rainbow, rainfall of sparkling gold

4) Who was the king of Sodom?
Bruton, Bera, Birsha, Ben

5) What Jewish sect did Jesus call a "generation of vipers"?
Pharisees, Essenes, Sadducees, Ebionites

6) Who became king of Judah after his father Manasseh's death?
Matri, Amon, Pildash, Tabeel

ANSWERS:

1) Neither. (Hannah was the mother of Samuel.)

2) Eve (Genesis 3: 13, 20).

3) Star (Matthew 2:7 – 10).

4) Bera (Genesis 14:2).

5) Pharisees (Mathew 23:29, 33).

6) Amon (2 Chronicles 33:9, 20 – 21).

Score Correct_____ Date_____ Name_____

*Study Notes:*_____

_____

Quiz 90

1) Is the book of Festus in the Old Testament, the New Testament, or neither?

2) In Deuteronomy, on referring to the Lord, "He is the ____, his work is perfect, a God of truth and without iniquity."
Just, rock, judge, answer

3) How many times in the Bible do the words Christian or Christians appear?
Three, thirteen, thirty, three hundred

4) After Ananias was sent to Saul by the Lord Jesus to lay his hands on him, what did Saul do after he received his sight?
Sing praises, drop to his knees, get baptized, look upward into the eyes of God

5) In Hebrews, it is impossible to please God without ____?
Love, faith, sorrow, tithing

6) How long do angels live, according to Jesus in Luke 20?
One year, ten thousand years, dependent on deeds, they never die

ANSWERS:

1) Neither. (Porcius Festus was a Roman governor in the reign of Nero.)

2) Rock (Deuteronomy 32:4).

3) Three (Acts 11:26, 26:28; 1 Peter 4:16).

4) Get baptized (Acts 9:17 – 18).

5) Faith (Hebrews 11:6).

6) They never die (Luke 20:34 – 36).

Score Correct_____ Date_____ Name _____
Study Notes:_____
_____

Samson Destroying the Temple of Dagon

Quiz 91

1) Is the book of Jephthah in the Old Testament, the New Testament, or neither?

2) From Jesus' words in Matthew 18, who beholds the face of God when someone hurts a little one?
Their angels, a mighty whisper, souls of their ancestors, the little one's thoughts

3) Who called herself Mara, a name meaning "bitter"?
Priscilla, Miriam, Naomi, Deborah

4) How many times is the first woman, Eve, mentioned by name in the Bible?
Two, four, seven, eleven

5) Where was king Josiah killed?
Megiddo, Anathoth, Philadelphia, Jericho

6) What did Malachi say the people of Judah were robbing, thus stealing from God?
Servants, unrighteous miracles, Holy Grail, owed tithes and offerings

ANSWERS:

1) Neither. (Jephthah was a Gileadite who became a judge in Israel for six years.)

2) Their angels (Matthew 18:10).

3) Naomi (Ruth 1:20).

4) Four (Genesis 3:20, 4:1; 1 Timothy 2:13; 2 Corinthians 11:3).

5) Megiddo (2 Kings 23:29).

6) Owed tithes and offerings (Malachi 3:4, 8).

Score Correct _____ Date_____ Name _____
Study Notes:_____
_____

Quiz 92

1) Is the book of Samaria in the Old Testament, the New Testament, or neither?

2) Who said, "Dead flies cause the ointment of the apothecary to send forth a stinking savour" (which may be translated as "Dead flies give perfume a bad smell")?
   Samson, Solomon, Samuel, Sargon

3) What creature or animal did Jesus compare Herod to?
   Swine, fox, locust, lion

4) Whose two wicked sons, Hophni and Phinehas, cared for the Ark of the Covenant at Shiloh?
   Elon, Eli, Ephai, Enau

5) The word "Messiah" means "anointed" and is only found in which book?
   Isaiah, Lamentations, Ezekiel, Daniel

6) In 1 Thessalonians, all brethren should be greeted with what?
   Praise to God, warm hearts, an holy kiss, open arms

ANSWERS:

1) Neither. (Samaria, in present day, is the territory generally known as part of the West Bank.)

2) Solomon (Ecclesiastes 1:1, 10:1).

3) Fox (Luke 13:31 – 32).

4) Eli (1 Samuel 4:3 – 4).

5) Daniel (Daniel 9:25 – 26). (Note: "Messias" is found in John 1:41 and John 4:25.)

6) An holy kiss (1 Thessalonians 5:26).

Score Correct _____ Date _____ Name _____
Study Notes: _____

_____

Quiz 93

1) Is the book of Tyre in the Old Testament, the New Testament, or neither?

2) Who is the first priest mentioned in the Bible?
   Adam, Melchizedek, Noah, Henoch

3) Which book of the Bible has the most mentions of the words "angel" or "angels"?
   Genesis, Psalms, Luke, Revelation

4) What is defined as the substance of things hoped for, the evidence of things not seen?
   Belief, faith, glory, church

5) In James 2, "Thou shalt love thy neighbour as thyself." is called the _____ law?
   Heavenly, first, highest, royal

6) What did Isaiah say the Lord likened sin to what color?
   Black as darkness, orange as glowing, red like crimson, green like envy

ANSWERS:
1) Neither. (Tyre is a coastal city of Phoenicia, now Lebanon.)
2) Melchizedek (Genesis 14:18).
3) Revelation (with 75).
4) Faith (Hebrews 11:1).
5) Royal (James 2:8).
6) Red like crimson (Isaiah 1:18).

Score Correct_____ Date_____ Name _____
Study Notes:_____
_____

Quiz 94

1) Is the book of Zechariah in the Old Testament, the New Testament, or neither?

2) King Solomon had a navy which returned every three years bringing gold, silver, ivory, and what animals?
Horses and camels, birds and elephants, apes and peacocks, chickens and sheep

3) Who did Paul refer to as his son in the faith?
Onesimus, Mark, Tychicus, Timothy

4) How many times is the word "demon" specifically mentioned in the Bible?
Zero, six, seventeen, fifty-two

5) Who conquered thirty-one kings and their lands in one campaign because the Lord fought for Israel?
David, Joshua, Jehozabad, Maasiai

6) In 2 Kings, a desperate woman boiled and ate her _____?
Arm, dog, ailing father, son

ANSWERS:

1) Old Testament. (Zechariah is the thirty-eighth and next-to-last book of the Old Testament.)

2) Apes and peacocks (1 Kings 10:21 – 22).

3) Timothy (1 Timothy 1:1 – 2).

4) Zero. (Other words and phrases such as devils and unclean spirits are utilized.)

5) Joshua (Joshua 12: 7 – 24).

6) Son (2 Kings 6:28 – 29).

Score Correct _____ Date_____ Name _____
Study Notes: _____
_____

Quiz 95

1) Is the book of 3 Samuel in the Old Testament, the New Testament, or neither?

2) In Genesis 3, to whom did God ask, "Who told thee that thou wast naked"?
   Eve, Cain, Adam, Moses

3) What five-year-old boy was dropped by his nurse and lamed for life?
   Moses, Mephibosheth, Peter, Andronicus

4) Which verse of the Bible contains every letter of the alphabet?
   Isaiah 1:1, Ezra 7:21, Amos 17:20, Joel 4:18

5) What did Jesus say a father would never give to his son instead of a fish?
   Stone, staff, song, serpent

6) In Judges 16, who said, "Let me die with the Philistines."?
   Delilah, Samson, Lot, Enos

ANSWERS:

1) Neither. (3 Samuel is fictitious, but 1 and 2 Samuel are the ninth and tenth books of the Old Testament.)

2) Adam (Genesis 3:9 – 11).

3) Mephibosheth (2 Samuel 4:4).

4) Ezra 7:21.

5) Serpent (Luke 11:11).

6) Samson (Judges 16:30).

Score Correct _____ Date _____ Name _____

Study Notes: _____

_____

Quiz 96

1) Is the book of Dorcas in the Old Testament, the New Testament, or neither?

2) In Deuteronomy, a woman wearing men's clothing is _____unto the Lord?
   Abomination, hateful, dung, vile

3) Who traveled to Corinth to help pick up an offering for needy saints?
   Vitas, Timothy, Philemon, Titus

4) Fill in the blank from Proverbs: "A fool despiseth his _____ instruction: but he that regardeth reproof is prudent."
   Priest's, father's, sin's, brethren's

5) In Leviticus, "To be cut off from the people" was the penalty of doing what?
   Whoring after wizards, bowing to idols, conducting stonings, public dancing

6) Who never died, as he was taken up to heaven in a whirlwind?
   Elishaphat, Elijah, Elizur, Elkanah

ANSWERS:

1) Neither. (Dorcas, also known as Tabitha, was raised from the dead by Peter.)

2) Abomination (Deuteronomy 22:5).

3) Titus (2 Corinthians 8:6 – 19).

4) Father's (Proverbs 15:5).

5) Whoring after wizards (Leviticus 20:2, 6).

6) Elijah (2 Kings 2:11).

Score Correct_____ Date_____ Name _____
Study Notes: _____
_____

Quiz 97

1) Is the book of Cain in the Old Testament, the New Testament, or neither?

2) Who was the wife of Nabal, the man who was churlish and evil in his doings?
   Abigail, Basemeth, Salome, Timnah

3) Who was king of Gerar?
   Abimelech, Nathan, Nehemiah, Joash

4) What did Simon's wife's mother lay sick of before Jesus healed her?
   Shakes, blindness, leprosy, fever

5) In the book of Numbers, a man was stoned to death for doing what on the Sabbath day?
   Singing too loud, gathering sticks, washing his ass (donkey), killing a serpent

6) Fill in the blank: "Therefore all things whatsoever ye would that men should do to you, do ye even so to them: for this is the law and the ____."
   Land, way, fortitude, prophets

ANSWERS:

1) Neither. (Cain was the eldest son of Adam and Eve who murdered his brother Abel.)

2) Abigail (1 Samuel 25:3).

3) Abimelech (Genesis 20:2).

4) Fever (Mark 1:30 – 31).

5) Gathering sticks (Numbers 15:32 – 36).

6) Prophets (Matthew 7:12, commonly called the Golden Rule).

Score Correct _____ Date _____ Name _____
Study Notes: _____

_____

Quiz 98

1) Is the book of 2 Corinthians in the Old Testament, the New Testament, or neither?

2) Who was king of Judah when the book of the law was found in the house of the Lord?
Amaziah, Josiah, Eglon, Joash

3) When Jesus came from Galilee to the river Jordan to be baptized by John, what was John's attitude?
Overjoyed, angry, sad, reluctant

4) Who was an instructor of working with brass and iron?
Nimrod, Tubalcain, Hezekiah, Manasseh

5) What two men in the Bible never died?
Noah and Moses, Enoch and Elijah, Peter and Paul, Kohath and Seba

6) The term "swaddling clothes" is specifically mentioned how many times in the Bible?
One, two, three, four

ANSWERS:

1) New Testament. (2 Corinthians is the eighth book of the New Testament.)

2) Josiah (2 Kings 22:3, 8 – 10).

3) Reluctant (Matthew 3:13 – 15).

4) Tubalcain (Genesis 4:22).

5) Enoch and Elijah (Genesis 5:24, 2 Kings 2:11).

6) Two (Luke 2:7, 12).

Score Correct _____ Date _____ Name _____

Study Notes: _____

Quiz 99

1) Is the book of Camon in the Old Testament, the New Testament, or neither?

2) In Matthew, what shall be preached in all the world before the end comes?
Word of God, gospel of the kingdom, peace to all, goodwill to humankind

3) According to Isaiah, what shall be the serpent's meat?
Lice, dust, fish, straw

4) Which book begins: "Paul, an apostle of Jesus Christ by the commandment of God our Saviour, and Lord Jesus Christ, which is our hope."?
1 Timothy, Titus, James, 2 John

5) Where did Moses die?
Shinar, Moab, Nod, Havilah

6) Why did Abraham construct a fire on top of Mount Moriah?
To signal God, to give warmth for his flock, to make a clearing for the hut, to sacrifice his son Isaac

ANSWERS:

1) Neither. (Camon was a town in Gilead where Jair died and was buried.)

2) Gospel of the kingdom (Matthew 24:14).

3) Dust (Isaiah 65:25).

4) 1 Timothy (1 Timothy 1:1).

5) Moab (Deuteronomy 34:5 – 7).

6) To sacrifice his son Isaac (Genesis 22:2, 6 – 7).

Score Correct _____ Date _____ Name _____

Study Notes: _____

_____

Quiz 100

1) Is the book of Abner in the Old Testament, the New Testament, or neither?

2) When the Lord spake unto Moses directing each Israelite counted in the census to give how much as an offering?
Half a shekel, one shekel, two shekels, four shekels

3) Who was the only woman Paul pointed out in his letter to Philemon?
Anna, Apphia, Cozbi, Damaris

4) In the book Matthew, Jesus said, "Go ye therefore, and teach all nations, _____ them in the name of the Father, and of the Son, and of the Holy Ghost."
Witnessing, praising, baptizing, instructing

5) What was Succothbenoth as made by the men of Babylon?
Public arena, false god, city gate, massive wall

6) According to the book of Acts, what title belonged to Agrippa?
Priest, apostle, king, general

ANSWERS:
1) Neither. (Abner was the son of Ner and king Saul's military commander.)
2) Half a shekel (Exodus 30:11 – 15).
3) Apphia (Philemon 1:1 – 2).
4) Baptizing (Matthew 28:19).
5) False god (2 Kings 17:30).
6) King (Acts 25:13, 24, 27).

Score Correct _____ Date_____ Name _____
Study Notes: _____
_____

Quiz 101

1) Is the book of Zimri in the Old Testament, the New Testament, or neither?

2) In Revelation, what perfectly square city is described as having walls made of jasper?
New Damascus, Jericho, New Jerusalem, Philadelphia

3) Who was the daughter of Saul that became David's first wife?
Shelomit, Michal, Bihah, Keziah

4) What two books in the Bible are named for women?
Naomi and Mary, Ruth and Esther, Deborah and Dorcas, Leah and Jael

5) Luke said Jesus was about how old when he began to teach?
Twenty, thirty, forty, fifty

6) In Philippians 4, what does the apostle Paul instruct us to do rather than worry?
Cry, pray, love, talk

ANSWERS:

1) Neither. (In the book of Numbers, Zimri was a prince among the Simeonites and slain by Phinehas.)

2) New Jerusalem (Revelation 21:2, 16 – 18).

3) Michal (1 Samuel 18:20 – 23).

4) Ruth and Esther. (In the Old Testament, Ruth is the eight book, Esther is the seventeenth.)

5) Thirty (Luke 3:23, 4:14 – 15).

6) Pray (Philippians 4:6 – 9).

Score Correct_____ Date_____ Name _____
*Study Notes:*_____

_____

Quiz 102

1) Is the book of Orpah in the Old Testament, the New Testament, or neither?
2) At what pool did Jesus heal a man of blindness by putting clay (mud) over his eyes?
   Shelah, Gibeon, Samaria, Siloam
3) Saul consented to the death of which Christian martyr?
   Andrew, Mark, Stephen, Thomas
4) Which of these was not a son of Ham, and thus not among the grandsons of Noah?
   Cush, Mizraim, Darda, Canaan
5) Fill in the blank from Simon Peter's confession: "Thou art the Christ, the Son of the ____ God."
   Heavenly, eternal, repenting, living
6) Which of the seven "preachers" referred to in Acts 6 went to the city of Samaria and advocated Christ unto them?
   Philip, Prochorus, Nicanor, Timon

ANSWERS:

1) Neither. (Orpah was the daughter-in-law of Naomi and sister-in-law of Ruth.)
2) Siloam (John 9:11).
3) Stephen (Acts 7:58 – 59, 8:1).
4) Darda (Genesis 5:32, 10:6).
5) Living (Matthew 16:16).
6) Philip (Acts 6:5, 8:4 – 5).

Score Correct_____ Date_____ Name _____
Study Notes:_____
_____

Quiz 103

1) Is the book of Ephesians in the Old Testament, the New Testament, or neither?

2) Matthew 7:15, Mark 13:22, and 1 John 4:1 are among many verses in the Bible that warn about what?
Love of money, false prophets, not tithing, immorality

3) Who was the king of Gomorrah?
Bruton, Bera, Birsha, Ben

4) What title of the Messiah was foretold by Isaiah in the Old Testament, "The Prince of _____."?
Love, All, Peace, Kindness

5) Where was Rachel, Jacob's wife, buried on the way to?
Dalmatia, Neah, Ephrath, Rissah

6) From the book Ephesians, "For we are members of his body, of his flesh, and of his _____."?
Witness, bones, love, life

ANSWERS:

1) New Testament. (Ephesians is the tenth book of the New Testament.)

2) False prophets (called among other things, ravening wolves).

3) Birsha (Genesis 14:2).

4) Peace (Isaiah 9:6).

5) Ephrath (Genesis 35:15 – 16, 19).

6) Bones (Ephesians 5:30).

Score Correct_____ Date_____ Name _____

*Study Notes:*_____

_____

Quiz 104

1) Is the book of Hapharaim in the Old Testament, the New Testament, or neither?

2) How much hotter than normal did king Nebuchadnezzar order the fiery furnace when he commanded Shadrach, Meshach, and Abednego be cast into it?
   Two times, three times, five times, seven times

3) Who was the sorcerer and false prophet at Paphos that Paul struck blind for his heresy?
   Ambrose, Isidore, Bede, Barjesus

4) From the book of Hebrews "Jesus is titled the _____ and finisher of our faith."?
   Beginning, endurer, author, shepherd

5) Whose name means a father of many nations?
   Adam, Noah, Methuselah, Abraham

6) Who secretly inspected the gates and walls of Jerusalem as they were in ruins?
   Manaen, Shemeber, Nehemiah, Tanhumeth

ANSWERS:

1) Neither. (Hapharaim was a city mentioned in Joshua 19:19.)
2) Seven times (Daniel 3:19 – 20).
3) Barjesus (Elymas by interpretation; Acts 13:6 – 11).
4) Author (Hebrews 12:2).
5) Abraham (Genesis 17:5).
6) Nehemiah (Nehemiah 2:11 – 16).

Score Correct _____ Date _____ Name _____

Study Notes: _____

_____

Quiz 105

1) Is the book of Hagar in the Old Testament, the New Testament, or neither?

2) Jesus said, "Go ye therefore, and teach all nations, baptizing them in the name of the Father, and of the Son, and of the Holy _____."
   Man, Church, Grail, Ghost

3) Who advised listeners to stop thinking like children?
   Luke, Paul, David, John

4) During one of the plagues of Egypt, when did the Pharaoh say he wanted the frogs to go away?
   Now, by sunset, tomorrow, never

5) How long did Paul stay in Corinth teaching the word of God?
   One month, a year, a year and six months, three years

6) Which was not one of the three times a day the Psalmist prayed and called upon God?
   Evening, morning, noon, two hours before sunset

ANSWERS:

1) Neither. (Hagar was Sarah's handmaid who became Abraham's wife.)

2) Ghost (Matthew 28:19).

3) Paul (1 Corinthians 3:5, 14:20).

4) Tomorrow (Exodus 8:9 – 10).

5) A year and six months (Acts 18:1, 11).

6) Two hours before sunset (Psalm 55:16 – 17).

Score Correct _____ Date _____ Name _____

Study Notes: _____

_____

Quiz 106

1) Is the book of 2 John in the Old Testament, the New Testament, or neither?
2) What did king Jehosophat make an arrangement to build with king Ahaziah that were later destroyed by the Lord?
Walls, chariots, idols, ships
3) As all sins are created equal, whoever hateth his brother is _____?
A murderer, unloved, a bad person, unforgiven
4) What word occurs frequently at the end of a verse in Psalms (over seventy times) and Habakkuk (three times), probably as a musical direction?
Simba, Selah, Sando, Sumed
5) How many chariots did king Solomon possess, as stated in 1 Kings 10?
130, 560, 1180, 1400
6) How were Moses' father and mother related?
Uncle and niece, nephew and aunt, brother-in-law and sister-in-law, first cousins

ANSWERS:

1) New Testament. (2 John is the twenty-fourth book of the New Testament.)
2) Ships (2 Chronicles 20:35 – 37).
3) A murderer (1 John 3:15).
4) Selah (Numerous times in Psalms, Habakkuk 3:3, 9, 13).
5) 1400 (1 Kings 10:26).
6) Nephew and aunt (Exodus 6:20).

Score Correct_____ Date_____ Name _____
Study Notes: _____

Quiz 107

1) Is the book of Jehu in the Old Testament, the New Testament, or neither?
2) King Jehoram was inflicted with a great sickness in what part of his body?
   Feet, eyes, hands, bowels
3) Who or what was Shishak?
   Roasted lamb, birthplace of Moses, serpent's name, king of Egypt
4) In Matthew 4, how many days and nights did Jesus fast before his temptation by Satan?
   Three, twelve, forty, seven times seventy
5) What was the name of the god of the men of Babylon?
   Ashima, Succothbenoth, Nergal, Adrammelech
6) Who said, "The Lord gave, and the Lord hath taken away; blessed be the name of the Lord."?
   Adam, Job, Haman, Jannes

ANSWERS:

1) Neither. (Jehu was a son of Hanani and known for driving chariots like a madman.)
2) Bowels (2 Chronicles 21: 15 – 18).
3) King of Egypt (1 Kings 11:40).
4) Forty (Matthew 4:1 – 2).
5) Succothbenoth (2 Kings 17:29 – 30).
6) Job (Job 1:21).

Score Correct_____ Date_____ Name _____
Study Notes: _____
_____

Quiz 108

1) Is the book of Jubal in the Old Testament, the New Testament, or neither?
2) What city had so many idols and false gods they even made an altar "To the Unknown God"?
   Gomorrah, Sidon, Babylon, Athens
3) In Revelation, what will the Lion of the tribe of Juda loose?
   Life, everlasting torment, Death, the seven seals
4) Which book begins by stating both the prophet's time and his roots?
   Nahum, Jonah, Zephaniah, Malachi
5) In Proverbs, what is held up as an example to the lazy man?
   Bee, flea, locust, ant
6) Who read the words of Jeremiah when the people of Jerusalem gathered for a fast before the Lord?
   Josiah, Gemariah, Baruch, Elnathan

ANSWERS:
1) Neither. (Jubal was the younger son of Adah and is considered the father of all musicians.)
2) Athens (Acts 17:16, 23).
3) The seven seals (Revelation 5:5).
4) Zephaniah (Zephaniah 1:1).
5) Ant (Proverbs 6:6).
6) Baruch (Jeremiah 36:9 – 10).

Score Correct _____ Date _____ Name _____
Study Notes: _____
_____

Quiz 109

1) Is the book of 2 Thessalonians in the Old Testament, the New Testament, or neither?
2) Who were rebuked by the disciples but said by Jesus to be the true possessors of heaven?
   Sheepherders, little children, redeemed harlots, honest moneychangers
3) In Revelation 12, who fights against Satan?
   Gabriel, the Angel of the Lord, cherubims, Michael and his angels
4) The Philistines, as an enemy of Israel, stole the Ark of the Covenant and were cursed with calamities for how many months?
   Seven, eighteen, twenty-five, fifty
5) Who shut the door of Noah's ark?
   His wife, Noah, the Lord, Abraham
6) Fill in the blank from the book of John: "He that eateth bread with me hath lifted up his _____ against me."
   Life, trust, fury, heel

ANSWERS:
1) New Testament. (2 Thessalonians is the fourteenth book of the New Testament.)
2) Little children (Matthew 19:13 – 14).
3) Michael and his angels (Revelation 12:7 – 9).
4) Seven (1 Samuel 5:11 – 12, 6:1).
5) The Lord (Genesis 7:16).
6) Heel (John 13:18, also Psalm 41:9).

Score Correct_____ Date_____ Name _____
*Study Notes:*_____
_____

Elijah Ascends to Heaven in a Chariot of Fire

Quiz 110

1) Is the book of Nehemiah in the Old Testament, the New Testament, or neither?

2) Commanding demons to leave other people was practiced by various people; how many times are the words "exorcist" or "exorcists" specifically mentioned in the Bible?
Zero, one, seven, twelve

3) Who was a hairy man, girt with a girdle of leather about his loins?
Adonai, Elijah, Malachi, Ashkenaz

4) What did Moses cast into the bitter water at Marah to make it sweet?
Hare, rock, robe, tree

5) What did Samson use as a weapon to slay a thousand men?
Spear of Gath, heavy oak branch, jawbone of an ass (donkey), bands of silver

6) Where were Paul and Barnabas proclaimed as gods after the healing of a crippled man?
Lystra, Myra, Nicopolis, Erech

ANSWERS:

1) Old Testament. (Nehemiah is the sixteenth book of the Old Testament.)
2) One (Acts 19:13).
3) Elijah (The Tishbite. 2 Kings 1:8).
4) Tree (Exodus 15:22 – 25).
5) Jawbone of an ass (donkey) (Judges 15:12 – 15).
6) Lystra (Acts 14:8 – 12).

Score Correct_____ Date_____ Name _____
Study Notes: _____
_____

Quiz 111

1) Is the book of Lamentations in the Old Testament, the New Testament, or neither?

2) Fill in the blank from 1 Peter: "Be sober, be vigilant; because your adversary the devil, as a roaring lion, walketh about, seeking whom he may _____."
Convince, devour, ravage, desolate

3) What city mentioned in Joshua 19 is the present-day Yaroun, Lebanon?
Cobalt, Curium, Zinc, Iron

4) Who or what did Adam blame for his eating of the forbidden fruit in the Garden of Eden?
Serpent, tree, his hunger, the woman

5) In the book of Matthew, who was Jesus' earthly grandfather?
Sargon, Medan, Gareb, Jacob

6) How long did Isaiah walk around naked and barefoot for a sign and wonder?
One week, forty days, one hundred days, three years

ANSWERS:

1) Old Testament. (Lamentations is the twenty-fifth book of the Old Testament.)

2) Devour (1 Peter 5:8).

3) Iron (Joshua 19:38).

4) The woman (Genesis 3:12).

5) Jacob (Matthew 1:16).

6) Three years (Isaiah 20:3).

Score Correct _____ Date _____ Name _____

Study Notes: _____

_____

Quiz 112

1) Is the book of 2 Kings in the Old Testament, the New Testament, or neither?
2) Mark quoted Jesus as saying, "For every one shall be salted with _____, and every sacrifice shall be salted with salt." Worms, miracles, fire, clouds
3) Ezekiel saw visions of God above what body of water? Sea of Galilee, Jordan River, Red Sea, River of Chebar
4) In the book of Genesis, who had a dream about kine (cows) coming up out of the river and standing by the riverside? Laban, Pharaoh, Jacob, Joseph
5) Jesus referred to the scribes and Pharisees as hypocrites and a generation of what? Adulterers, weeds, wolves, vipers
6) According to Paul in 1 Corinthians, what is the greatest of enduring virtues? Faith, hope, charity, honesty

ANSWERS:
1) Old Testament. (2 Kings is the twelfth book of the Old Testament.)
2) Fire (Mark 9:49).
3) River of Chebar (Ezekiel 1:1).
4) Pharaoh (Genesis 41:1 – 3).
5) Vipers (Matthew 23:29 – 33).
6) Charity (1 Corinthians 13:13).

Score Correct_____ Date_____ Name _____
Study Notes:_____

_____

Quiz 113

1) Is the book of Lazarus in the Old Testament, the New Testament, or neither?

2) From 1 Kings, what prophet experienced an earthquake while standing on a mountaintop?
   Paul, Ahab, Andrew, Elijah

3) Who was Menahem's son who ruled for two years in Samaria and then killed by his army captain, Pekah?
   Shallum, Pekahiah, Jehoahaz, Nadab

4) What word found only in 1 Chronicles possibly means a row of pillars or colonnade?
   Ignominy, pare, unction, parbar

5) Who was the sorcerer and false prophet at Paphos that Paul struck blind for his heresy?
   Ambrose, Isidore, Bede, Barjesus

6) What king of Judah burned the book of Jeremiah strip by strip as it was read to him?
   Rehoboam, Jehoiakim, Ahaziah, Zedekiah

ANSWERS:

1) Neither. (Lazarus was the man raised from the dead by Jesus.)

2) Elijah (1 Kings 19:11 – 13).

3) Pekahiah (2 Kings 15:22 – 26).

4) Parbar (1 Chronicles 26:18).

5) Barjesus (Elymas by interpretation; Acts 13:6 – 11).

6) Jehoiakim (Jeremiah 36:23 – 29).

Score Correct _____ Date _____ Name _____

Study Notes: _____

_____

Quiz 114

1) Is the book of Leviticus in the Old Testament, the New Testament, or neither?

2) In Deuteronomy, one should not plow with an ox and what other animal yoked together?
   Camel, bear, ass (donkey), antelope

3) Who was the father of Mahlah, Hoglah, Milcah, Tirzah, and Noah?
   Abialbon, Helkai, Laadan, Zelophehad

4) Who was Manasseh's son who ruled two years in Jerusalem and then killed by his own servants?
   Jotham, Amon, Hezekiah, Elah

5) In Exodus 16, what bird served as food for the Israelites in the wilderness?
   Dove, quail, duck, robin

6) The Bible does not say that money is the root of all evil; instead it says the _____ of money is.
   Hoarding, spending, love, lust

ANSWERS:

1) Old Testament. (Leviticus is the third book of the Old Testament.)
2) Ass (donkey) (Deuteronomy 22:10).
3) Zelophehad (Numbers 26:33, 27:1).
4) Amon (2 Kings 21:18 – 23).
5) Quail (Exodus 16:12 – 13).
6) Love (1 Timothy 6:10).

Score Correct_____ Date_____ Name _____
Study Notes:_____
_____

Quiz 115

1) Is the book of Canaan in the Old Testament, the New Testament, or neither?

2) Jesus once told a group of Pharisees and Sadducees, "When it is evening, ye say, it will be fair weather for the sky is _____."
Darkened, blue, red, swirling

3) Who did the Lord make for the day of evil?
The wicked, harlots, the naughty, mockers

4) Demetrius was a silversmith who made silver shrines of what false goddess?
Diana, Asherah, Ishtar, Anammelech

5) In the book of Acts, what trade did Simon practice in Samaria?
Medicine, sorcery, coppersmithing, tentmaking

6) Who served an angel a kid (young goat) in a basket and put the broth in a pot?
Paul, Gideon, John the Baptist, Luke

ANSWERS:
1) Neither. (Canaan was a son of Ham and grandson of Noah.)
2) Red (Matthew 16:1 – 2).
3) The wicked (Proverbs 16:4).
4) Diana (Acts 19:24).
5) Sorcery (Acts 8:5 – 9).
6) Gideon (Judges 6:19 – 20).

Score Correct _____ Date _____ Name _____
Study Notes: _____
_____

Quiz 116

1) Is the book of Eve in the Old Testament, the New Testament, or neither?

2) Who cut off the gold from the doors of the temple of the Lord and gave it to the king of Assyria?
Jotham, Hezekiah, Ahaz, Menahem

3) From Psalm 62, "In God is my salvation and my glory: the _____ of my strength, and my refuge."
Hope, wall, rock, captain

4) What prophet was imprisoned into the muddy dungeon of Malchiah?
Amos, Joel, Huldah, Jeremiah

5) Where was Saul publicly proclaimed king?
Tekoa, Gilgal, Netophah, Yavne

6) Who stuck his javelin into the wall when it failed to strike David, its intended target?
Saul, Goliath, Solomon, Abel

ANSWERS:

1) Neither. (Eve was the wife of Adam and humankind's first woman.)

2) Hezekiah (2 Kings 18:16).

3) Rock (Psalm 62:7).

4) Jeremiah (Jeremiah 38:6).

5) Gilgal (1 Samuel 11:14 – 15).

6) Saul (1 Samuel 19:10).

Score Correct_____ Date_____ Name _____
Study Notes:_____
_____

Quiz 117

1) Is the book of Galatians in the Old Testament, the New Testament, or neither?

2) In 1 Chronicles, Elhanan, the son of Jair, slew the _____ of Goliath the Gittite?
Father, brother, king, oxen

3) Where did Timothy have troubles for which Paul advised a little wine?
Back, stomach, head, legs

4) Who tore his clothes when he heard his sons and daughters had all died when a great wind smote the house where they were eating?
David, Job, Daniel, Herod

5) In Matthew, what did Jesus say not to use when we pray?
Loud curses, impure thoughts, vain repetitions, wandering shifts

6) In what city did king Ahasuerus sit on the throne of his kingdom?
Kabzeel, Shushan, Antioch, Tarsus

ANSWERS:

1) New Testament. (Galatians is the ninth book of the New Testament.)

2) Brother (Named Lahmi; 1 Chronicles 20:5).

3) Stomach (1 Timothy 5:23).

4) Job. (Job 1:18 – 20. Note: rent means tore and mantle means clothing.)

5) Vain repetitions (Matthew 6:7).

6) Shushan (Esther 1:2).

Score Correct_____ Date_____ Name _____
Study Notes:_____
_____

Quiz 118

1) Is the book of Song of Solomon in the Old Testament, the New Testament, or neither?

2) Who was praised for his beauty "from the sole of his foot even to the crown of his head"?
Absalom, Elisha, Pekah, Tola

3) In Proverbs, what will pluck out the eyes of anyone who scorns their parents?
Demons, ravens, doves, quails

4) Who was the father of Hosea?
Uzzah, Beeri, Joash, Ahab

5) When Jesus entered into Capernaum, what Roman official asked him to heal his servant?
Marshall, governor, centurion, jailor

6) How many times are the words "apple" or "apples" mentioned in the Bible?
Eleven, fourteen, nineteen, thirty-seven

ANSWERS:

1) Old Testament. (Song of Solomon is the twenty-second book of the Old Testament.)

2) Absalom (a son of David; 2 Samuel 14:25).

3) Ravens (Proverbs 30:17).

4) Beeri (Hosea 1:1)

5) Centurion (Matthew 8:5 – 7).

6) Eleven (Deuteronomy 32:10; Psalms 17:8; Proverbs 7:2, 25:11; Song of Solomon 2:3, 2:5, 7:8, 8:5; Lamentations 2:18; Joel 1:12; Zechariah 2:8).

Score Correct_____ Date_____ Name _____
Study Notes: _____
_____

Quiz 119

1) Is the book of Malachi in the Old Testament, the New Testament, or neither?

2) When the sixth seal was opened in Revelation, what color was the sun when it became as sackcloth of hair?
Red, black, white, green

3) What camp saw 185,000 of its soldiers slaughtered by an angel of the Lord?
Assyrians, Midianites, Israelites, Philistines

4) In Acts 6, who did great wonders and miracles among the people?
Parmenas, Philip, Timon, Stephen,

5) What is the first color specifically mentioned in the Bible?
Purple, red, green, yellow

6) In 2 Kings, who became king at age eight and reigned in Jerusalem thirty-one years?
Abijam, Rehoboam, Marcus, Josiah

ANSWERS:

1) Old Testament. (Malachi is the thirty-ninth and last book of the Old Testament.)

2) Black (Revelation 6:12).

3) Assyrians (2 Kings 19:35).

4) Stephen (Acts 6:5 – 8).

5) Green (Genesis 1:30).

6) Josiah (2 Kings 22:1, also 2 Chronicles 34:1).

Score Correct _____ Date_____ Name _____

Study Notes:_____

Quiz 120

1) Is the book of Kezia in the Old Testament, the New Testament, or neither?

2) When the Lord spake unto Moses directing each Israelite to be counted in the census, what was the age and above to give an offering?
   Twelve, sixteen, twenty, twenty-one

3) Who was released before Pontius Pilate sentenced Jesus to death?
   Barabbas, Cosam, Onesiphorus, Shemiramoth

4) In Revelation, what color horse did Faithful and True ride?
   Red, white, black, blue

5) Who condemns drinkers who start early in the morning?
   Job, Isaiah, Ezra, Esther

6) In Ephesians, what did Paul recommend as a substitute for wine?
   Water, laughter, love, Spirit

ANSWERS:

1) Neither. (Kezia was a daughter of Job.)
2) Twenty (Exodus 30:11 – 14).
3) Barabbas (John 18:38 – 40; Luke 23:18).
4) White (Revelation 19:11).
5) Isaiah (Isaiah 5:11).
6) Spirit (Ephesians 5:18).

Score Correct_____ Date_____ Name _____
*Study Notes:*_____
_____

Quiz 121

1) Is the book of Absalom in the Old Testament, the New Testament, or neither?

2) Jesus originally selected twelve apostles, then Matthias became number thirteen to replace Judas, and who was called upon to be the fourteenth?
   Justus, Mark, Paul, John the Baptist

3) What son of Baasha, who reigned over Israel in Tirzah, was killed while drunk?
   Ahaziah, Elah, Jehoahaz, Asa

4) Two biblical characters ate a scroll and said that God's words tasted as sweet as honey; one was Ezekiel, and who was the other?
   Silas, John, Lucius, Simon

5) Which of the twelve tribes of Israel was exempt from going forth to war?
   Reuben, Levi, Simeon, Judah

6) Who forbade Paul and Timotheus (Timothy) to minister in Asia and Bithynia?
   Holy Spirit, Eunice, Silas, Lois

ANSWERS:
1) Neither. (Absalom was the third and favorite son of David.)
2) Paul (Matthew 10:2 – 4, Acts 1:26, Romans 1:1).
3) Elah (1 Kings 16:8 – 10).
4) John (Ezekiel 3:1 – 3, Revelation 10:9 – 10).
5) Levi (Genesis 49:28, Numbers 1:45 – 47).
6) Holy Spirit (Acts 16:1 – 7).

Score Correct _____ Date_____ Name _____
Study Notes:_____
_____

Quiz 122

1) Is the book of Mark in the Old Testament, the New Testament, or neither?

2) When Boaz discovered Ruth at his feet after he went to lie down, he was impressed because she had not followed a _____?
   Young man, drifter, tax collector, sheepherder

3) Who were the inhabitants of Jerusalem before David captured it?
   Galileans, Palestinians, Hittites, Jebusites

4) From Hebrews: "For the word of God is quick, and powerful, and _____ than any two-edged sword."
   Swifter, scarier, sharper, surgeful

5) What specifically-mentioned type of lizard was not permitted on Israelite menus as unclean?
   Gekko, chameleon, dragon, iguana

6) Jesus said, "But whosoever shall say, Thou fool, shall be in danger of _____."?
   Old time, hell fire, thine oaths, perfect punishment

ANSWERS:

1) New Testament. (Mark is the second book of the New Testament.)
2) Young man (Ruth 3:7 – 10).
3) Jebusites (2 Samuel 5:4 – 9).
4) Sharper (Hebrews 4:12).
5) Chameleon (Leviticus 11:29 – 30).
6) Hell fire (Matthew 5:22).

Score Correct_____ Date_____ Name _____
Study Notes: _____

_____

Quiz 123

1) Is the book of Joshua in the Old Testament, the New Testament, or neither?

2) At the battle in mount Gilboa, whose sons Jonathan, Abinadab, and Malchishua were slain by the Philistines?
Mathusala, Saul, Enan, Beninu

3) Who set out to glean in the fields after the reapers, to support her and her mother-in-law Naomi?
Dinah, Ruth, Julia, Syntyche

4) David was sure he could conquer Goliath, because as a shepherd he had smote both the lion and the_____?
Fox, bear, cobra, crocodile

5) What was the name of the god of the men of Cuth?
Ashima, Succothbenoth, Nergal, Adrammelech

6) In Luke, what animals were present at Jesus' birth?
Lions and bears, sheep and goats, cows and donkeys, no mention of animals

ANSWERS:

1) Old Testament. (Joshua is the sixth book of the Old Testament.)
2) Saul (1 Samuel 31:1 – 2).
3) Ruth (Ruth 2:2 – 9, 12).
4) Bear (1 Samuel 17:32 – 37).
5) Nergal (2 Kings 17:29 – 30).
6) No mention of animals (Luke 1:1 – 20).

Score Correct_____ Date_____ Name _____
Study Notes: _____
_____

Quiz 124

1) Is the book of Micah in the Old Testament, the New Testament, or neither?

2) When he fell into a trance and a voice came to him telling him to kill and eat, who said, "Not so, Lord; for I have never eaten any thing that is common or unclean."?
Adam, Reuben, Samson, Peter

3) Hegai was what king's chamberlain and keeper of the women?
Menaham, Ahasuerus, Shallum, Omri

4) In Proverbs, what type of men can bring a city into a snare, but wise men turn away wrath?
Scornful, greedy, winebibbing, bloodthirsty

5) In Matthew 16, every man shall be rewarded according to his _____?
Works, witnessing, way, family

6) Which of these fairly common words is only found once in the Bible?
Tabernacle, freedom, pathway, embalmed

ANSWERS:

1) Old Testament. (Micah is the thirty-third book of the Old Testament.)
2) Peter (Acts 10:9 – 14).
3) Ahasuerus (Esther 2:15 – 16).
4) Scornful (Proverbs 29:8).
5) Works (Matthew 16:27).
6) Pathway: Proverbs 12:28).

Score Correct_____ Date_____ Name _____
Study Notes:_____

Quiz 125

1) Is the book of Gilead in the Old Testament, the New Testament, or neither?

2) What is the only verse that contains the word "antichrist" and its plural, "antichrists"?
   Daniel 7:6, 1 Thessalonians 2:20, 1 John 2:18, Revelation 6:6

3) Who was the father of Esther and the uncle of Mordecai?
   Molid, Naarai, Zebina, Abihail

4) Who was churlish and evil in his doings, but had a clever wife, Abigail, of good understanding?
   Abitub, Chilion, Muppim, Nabal

5) What is described in scripture as "a fire, a world of iniquity"?
   Gomorrah, lustful desires, false prophets, the tongue

6) Mentioned only once in scripture, what safeguard contained a holy relic of parchments inscribed with verses that was worn on the body?
   Simlahs, etrogs, phylacteries, addereths

ANSWERS:

1) Neither. (Gilead is a mountainous region situated in modern-day Jordan.)

2) 1 John 2:18. ("Little children, it is the last time: and as ye have heard that antichrist shall come, even now are there many antichrists; whereby we know that it is the last time.")

3) Abihail (Esther 2:15).

4) Nabal (1 Samuel 25:3).

5) The tongue (James 3:6).

6) Phylacteries (Matthew 23:4 – 5).

Score Correct _____ Date_____ Name _____
Study Notes: _____
_____

Quiz 126

1) Is the book of Philippians in the Old Testament, the New Testament, or neither?

2) Who was the son of Solomon that took eighteen wives (with Maachah being his most loved) and threescore concubines?
Rehoboam, Mehujael, Anathoth, David

3) What cruel official had Zeresh as his wife?
Elkanah, Haman, Jucal, Hothir

4) From 2 Corinthians, every man should give according to his heart's purpose, as God loves what type of giver?
Smiling, cheerful, remorseful, unadulterated

5) Elijah's servant saw a little cloud arise out of the sea that looked like what?
Four sheets, ball of fire, a man's hand, seven chariots

6) When Isaiah foretold about the Messiah in the Old Testament, what did Isaiah say would be upon his shoulder?
The government, mankind, all righteousness, heavenly spirit

ANSWERS:

1) New Testament. (Philippians is the eleventh book of the New Testament.)

2) Rehoboam (2 Chronicles 11:21).

3) Haman (Esther 5:14).

4) Cheerful (2 Corinthians 9:7).

5) A man's hand (1 Kings 18:42 – 44).

6) The government (Isaiah 9:6).

Score Correct_____ Date_____ Name _____
Study Notes: _____
_____

Quiz 127

1) Is the book of Nathan in the Old Testament, the New Testament, or neither?

2) After coming ashore on the island in Melita, in whose house did Paul stay for three days?
   Aziel, Samlah, Publius, Raphu

3) Who had a son called Seth?
   Boaz and Ruth, Adam and Eve, Joseph and Mary, Jacob and Leah

4) What type of inheritance will the followers of Christ receive, one that will never _____?
   Tarry, fade, grow, hunger

5) In Luke, what term describes an army of angels praising God?
   Heavenly host, covenant, spirit multitude, Manoah

6) Moses stripped Aaron of his garments just before he died and put them on whom?
   Neariah, Eleazar, Rohgah, Tychicus

ANSWERS:
1) Neither. (Nathan was a son of David.)
2) Publius (Acts 28:1 – 7).
3) Adam and Eve (Genesis 4:25).
4) Fade (1 Peter 1:3 – 4).
5) Heavenly host (Luke 2:13).
6) Eleazar (his son; Numbers 20:28).

Score Correct _____ Date _____ Name _____

Study Notes: _____

_____

Job Hears of His Misfortunes

Quiz 128

1) Is the book of Obadiah in the Old Testament, the New Testament, or neither?

2) "Ashes to ashes, dust to dust," words commonly heard at graveside funerals, are adapted from God's words to whom?
Adam, Abraham, Moses, Noah

3) In 2 Thessalonians, the Antichrist is described as that man of sin, the son of _____?
Rebellion, perdition, Lucifer, greed

4) Before Jesus' first miracle of turning water into wine at a wedding in Cana, who saith unto him, "They have no wine."?
Anna, Mary, Joanna, Deborah

5) What angel appeared to Zacharias?
Raphael, Michael, Gabriel, an unnamed angel of the Lord

6) To whom did the Lord ask, "Where wast thou when I laid the foundations of the earth"?
Mark, the serpent, John the Baptist, Job

ANSWERS:

1) Old Testament. (Obadiah is the thirty-first book of the Old Testament.)

2) Adam (Genesis 3:17 – 19).

3) Perdition (2 Thessalonians 2:3).

4) Mary (John 2:1 – 3).

5) Gabriel (Luke 1:18 – 19).

6) Job (Job 38:1 – 4).

Score Correct _____ Date _____ Name _____

Study Notes: _____

_____

Quiz 129

1) Is the book of Obed in the Old Testament, the New Testament, or neither?
2) The word "Satan" is found nineteen times in the Old Testament, with fourteen mentions in which single book?
   1 Chronicles, Job, Psalms, Zechariah
3) Who was the goddess of Asia having a temple in Ephesus?
   Dagon, Hermes, Diana, Baal
4) Where did Moses bring water out of a rock?
   Horeb, Carmel, Pisgah, Gilboa
5) What did Sarah say she had not been doing, therefore lying to God?
   Walking, eating, laughing, lusting
6) Who was grateful for a gourd that shaded his head, thus delivering him from misery? Bartimaeus, Zophar, Moses, Jonah

ANSWERS:
1) Neither. (Obed was a son of Boaz, and the father of Jesse, and grandfather of David.)
2) Job (Job 1:6, 1:7, 1:8, 1:9, 1:12, 2:1, 2:2, 2:3, 2:4, 2:6, 2:7).
3) Diana (Acts 19:26 – 27).
4) Horeb (Exodus 17:6).
5) Laughing (Genesis 18:13 – 15).
6) Jonah (Jonah 4:6 – 7).

Score Correct _____ Date _____ Name _____
Study Notes: _____
_____

Quiz 130

1) Is the book of Esther in the Old Testament, the New Testament, or neither?

2) When a woman caught in adultery was brought to Jesus with a group assembled, what did Jesus write on the ground? It is not specified, the names of accusers, "forgiven," a list of her sins to be erased

3) From the book of Ecclesiastes, there is "a time to be born, and a time to _____"? Live, eat, die, praise

4) Who fled from Iconium unto Lystra and Derbe when they heard of a plot to stone them? Mary and Joseph, Paul and Barnabas, Samson and Delilah, Timothy and Titus

5) What is the one kind of woman a priest cannot marry? Harlot, divorcee, heathen, virgin

6) Some disciples were known by more than one name; what was Thomas's other name? Andrew, Didymus, Caleb, Zimri

ANSWERS:

1) Old Testament. (Esther is the seventeenth book of the Old Testament.)

2) It is not specified (John 8:3 – 8).

3) Die (Ecclesiastes 3:2).

4) Paul and Barnabas (Acts 13:50, 14:1 – 2, 5 – 6).

5) Divorcee (Ezekiel 44:21 – 22).

6) Didymus (John 11:16).

Score Correct_____ Date_____ Name _____
Study Notes:_____
_____

Quiz 131

1) Is the book of 2 Timothy in the Old Testament, the New Testament, or neither?

2) In Revelation, the beast was given a mouth to utter proud words and to exercise his authority for how many months? Forty-two, eighty-three, seven times seventy, one thousand

3) What was the first word spoken by Jesus as recorded in the New Testament? Peace, pray, forgive, suffer

4) In the beginning, how was the whole face of the ground watered before God sent rain? It wasn't, mist from the earth, God's breath, oceans rolling over land

5) Abigail, Michal, and Ahinoam were all wives of what person? Solomon, Peter, Obadiah, David

6) In the book of Matthew, what did Jesus say would not prevail against his church? Gates of hell, lust, evil forces, Satan's army

ANSWERS:

1) New Testament. (2 Timothy is the sixteenth book of the New Testament.)
2) Forty-two (Revelation 13:4 – 5).
3) Suffer (Matthew 3:15).
4) Mist from the earth (Genesis 2:5 – 6).
5) David (1 Samuel 25:40 – 44).
6) Gates of hell (Matthew 16:18).

Score Correct_____ Date_____ Name _____
Study Notes:_____

_____

Quiz 132

1) Is the book of Gemariah in the Old Testament, the New Testament, or neither?
2) When Moses parted the waters of the Red Sea, who moved from the front of the camp of Israel to the rear?
   Pharaoh, Ashbel, Hariph, Angel of God
3) In the book of Hebrews, what Old Testament priest was Jesus like?
   Melchisedec, Eli, Josiah, Abihu
4) The Lord will have war with whom from generation to generation?
   Hesbolah, Eliezer, Amalek, Pilate
5) Which book mentions the constellation Orion?
   Genesis, Exodus, Job, Jonah
6) What king slew the Gibeonites, breaking his promise of peace and angering God?
   Neco, Joash, Jehu, Saul

ANSWERS:

1) Neither. (Gemariah was a proper name applied to more than one individual including the son of Shaphan and the son of Hilkiah.)
2) Angel of God (Exodus 14:15 – 16, 19).
3) Melchisedec (Hebrews 5:5 – 6).
4) Amalek (Exodus 17:16).
5) Job (Job 9:8 – 9).
6) Saul (2 Samuel 21:1 – 2).

Score Correct_____ Date_____ Name _____
Study Notes: _____
_____

Quiz 133

1) Is the book of Issachar in the Old Testament, the New Testament, or neither?

2) What was Moses doing when God appeared to him in a flame of fire out of the midst of a bush?
Praying, sleeping, fishing, tending sheep

3) In 1 Corinthians, churches of _____ worshipped on the first day of the week?
Adventist, Galatia, Gideon, Balaam

4) Where did Jesus stay when John the Baptist was in prison?
Beersheba, Capernaum, Assos, Cana

5) From Proverbs 22: "A good name is rather to be chosen than great _____."
Riches, witness, corruption, love

6) An angel appearing in a dream told whom about the death of Herod?
Mary, Joseph, Matthias, Rachel

ANSWERS:

1) Neither. (Issachar was a son of Jacob.)
2) Tending sheep (Exodus 3:1 – 2).
3) Galatia (1 Corinthians 16:1 – 2).
4) Capernaum (Matthew 4:12 – 13).
5) Riches (Proverbs 22:1).
6) Joseph (Matthew 2:19).

Score Correct_____ Date_____ Name _____
Study Notes:_____

_____

Quiz 134

1) Is the book of Numbers in the Old Testament, the New Testament, or neither?
2) What prophet said, "The Lord also shall save the tents of Judah first."?
   Lamech, Zechariah, Jahaziel, Malachi
3) In John 3, what did Jesus compare the power of the Spirit to?
   Sea, wind, mountains, masses
4) The Antichrist shall not regard the desire of _____?
   Love, hunger, prisoners, women
5) Who was Moses' father-in-law?
   Jethro, Caleb, Abishur, Nahan
6) In the book of Mark, who asked, "Who touched my clothes"?
   Jesus, John the Baptist, David, Solomon

ANSWERS:
1) Old Testament. (Numbers is the fourth book of the Old Testament.)
2) Zechariah (Zechariah 12:7).
3) Wind (John 3:8).
4) Women (Daniel 11:36 – 37).
5) Jethro (Exodus 3:1).
6) Jesus (after a certain woman with an issue of blood twelve years; Mark 5:30).

Score Correct _____ Date _____ Name _____
Study Notes: _____
_____

Quiz 135

1) Is the book of 3 Corinthians in the Old Testament, the New Testament, or neither?

2) "Blessed is the man that endureth _____ for when he is tried, he shall receive the crown of life, which the Lord hath promised to them that love him."
Evil, temptation, sufferings, snares

3) From the book of Ecclesiastes, there is "a time to kill and a time to _____"?
Plant, embrace, heal, rest

4) What did Jesus say a man could forfeit, negating the gain of the whole world?
Life, love, house, soul

5) In Exodus, a shekel is how many gerahs?
Five, ten, fifteen, twenty

6) Though Eunice and the apostle Paul were not married to each other, they both called whom their son?
Timothy, Barnabas, Didymus, Mark

ANSWERS:

1) Neither. (3 Corinthians is fictitious, but 1 Corinthians and 2 Corinthians are the seventh and eighth books of the New Testament.)

2) Temptation (James 1:12).

3) Heal (Ecclesiastes 3:3).

4) Soul (Mark 8:36).

5) Twenty (Exodus 30:13).

6) Timothy (2 Timothy 1:1 – 5).

Score Correct_____ Date_____ Name _____
Study Notes:_____
_____

Quiz 136

1) Is the book of Hebrews in the Old Testament, the New Testament, or neither?
2) What suffereth long, is kind, envieth not, rejoiceth in the truth, and endureth all things?
   Goodness, charity, family, prayer
3) How many years will Jesus reign on earth before Satan's final judgment?
   Seven, fifty, one thousand, five thousand
4) As some disciples were known by more than one name, what was John's other name?
   Absalom, Mark, Benaiah, Arioch
5) How did Jesus instruct Judas to do his evil of betrayal?
   Abundantly, quickly, insincerely, peacefully
6) The book of Hebrews says to entertain strangers, as they may be _____?
   Demons, angels, prophets, reincarnated

ANSWERS:
1) New Testament. (Hebrews is the ninteenth book of the New Testament.)
2) Charity (Other translations say the scripture refers to love; 1 Corinthians 13:4 – 7).
3) One thousand (Revelation 20:6 – 10).
4) Mark (Acts 12:25).
5) Quickly (John 13:27).
6) Angels (Hebrews 13:2).

Score Correct_____ Date_____ Name _____
Study Notes: _____
_____

Quiz 137

1) Is the book of Dinah in the Old Testament, the New Testament, or neither?

2) Who asked to be thrown overboard during a bad windy storm, as the shipmaster and others thought this person had brought the evil upon them?
   Paul, Jonah, Aristarchus, Marcus

3) The river that watered the Garden of Eden was divided into how many heads?
   Two, four, dozens, hundreds

4) The Antichrist, as deceiver of miracles, will cause all to receive a mark in their right hand, or in their _____?
   Souls, necks, elbows, foreheads

5) Who/what killed the obese king Eglon of Moab?
   River Jordan, Abishai, Red Sea, Ehud

6) From Proverbs, he that hath no rule over his own spirit is like a _____ that is broken down?
   House, city, cart, fence

ANSWERS:

1) Neither. (Dinah was the daughter of Jacob and Leah.)
2) Jonah (Jonah 1:12 – 15).
3) Four (Genesis 2:10 – 14).
4) Foreheads (Revelation 13:14 – 16).
5) Ehud (Judges 3:17 – 21).
6) City (Proverbs 25:28).

Score Correct _____ Date _____ Name _____
Study Notes: _____
_____

Quiz 138

1) Is the book of Habakkuk in the Old Testament, the New Testament, or neither?
2) When Jesus was bearing his cross, he went forth into Golgotha, called the place of a _____?
   Dead, dog, skull, harlot
3) In Genesis 2, who named the animals?
   God, Serpent, Adam, Eve
4) Who or what killed Abner, the son of Ner and commander-in-chief of Saul's army?
   North wind, Joab, his own sword, Baalis
5) In Luke's gospel, what does Jesus compare the fall of Satan to?
   Door slamming, lightning, sheep off a cliff, bones snapping
6) Which of these fairly common words is found only in one verse of the Bible?
   Twinkling, villain, snake, Christmas

ANSWERS:
1) Old Testament. (Habakkuk is the thirty-fifth book of the Old Testament.)
2) Skull (John 19:16 – 17).
3) Adam (Genesis 2:19 – 20).
4) Joab (2 Samuel 3:27).
5) Lightning (Luke 10:18).
6) Twinkling. (1 Corinthians 15:52. Note: the other three choices not found in any verse.)

Score Correct _____ Date _____ Name _____
Study Notes: _____
_____

Quiz 139

1) Is the book of Ruth in the Old Testament, the New Testament, or neither?

2) Who was first of the twelve disciples to be murdered, by Herod the king with a sword?
Peter, Thomas, James, Judas

3) In the gospel of John, what was "in the beginning"?
The Earth, the Heavens, the Word, the Spirit

4) Who came to Jesus under the cover of night and asked, "How can a man be born when he is old?"
Elijah, Amos, Nicodemus, Mesha

5) How many people did Jesus himself baptize?
None, one, hundreds, thousands

6) What name did Jesus give to Simon Peter, which is, by interpretation, a stone?
Macedonia, Nahu, Cephas, Eli

ANSWERS:

1) Old Testament. (Ruth is eighth book of the Old Testament and is one of only two books named for women. Esther is the other.)

2) James (Acts 12:1 – 2).

3) The Word (John 1:1).

4) Nicodemus (John 3:1 – 4).

5) None (John 4:2).

6) Cephas (John 1:42).

Score Correct_____ Date_____ Name _____
Study Notes:_____
_____

Quiz 140

1) Is the book of Luke in the Old Testament, the New Testament, or neither?

2) In Revelation, how were both the beast and the false prophet cast into a lake of burning fire?
   Regretfully, hastily, upon death, alive

3) Who came to Jesus, said, "Hail, master," and kissed him?
   Alexander, Mark, Mordecai, Judas

4) From the book of Ecclesiastes, there is "a time to break down and a time to _____"?
   Plow, climb, rejoice, build up

5) Which of these was a son of Nun?
   Jehoshaphat, Joshua, Zacchaeus, Meshach

6) To whom did God say, "Before I formed thee in the belly I knew thee . . . and I ordained thee a prophet unto the nations."?
   Daniel, Jeremiah, Noah, Thomas

ANSWERS:

1) New Testament. (Luke is the third book of the New Testament.)

2) Alive (Revelation 19:20).

3) Judas (Matthew 26:47 – 49).

4) Build up (Ecclesiastes 3:3).

5) Joshua (Exodus 33:11, Numbers 11:28).

6) Jeremiah (Jeremiah 1:1 – 5).

Score Correct _____ Date _____ Name _____

Study Notes: _____

_____

Quiz 141

1) Is the book of Manasseh in the Old Testament, the New Testament, or neither?

2) The plague of insects described in the book of Joel does not specifically mention which of these?
   Palmerworm, bristleworm, cankerworm, caterpillar

3) How far of a journey from Jerusalem was the mount called Olivet?
   Sabbath's day, three days and a half, one week, one month

4) How many years did David reign over all Israel?
   Seven, thirty-three, forty, fifty-seven

5) On what isle was John given the book of Revelation in a vision?
   Chittim, Tarshish, Elishah, Patmos

6) How many shekels did Absalom's hair weigh after he polled (cut) it off at every year's end?
   Two, ten, fifty, two hundred

ANSWERS:

1) Neither. (Manasseh was the firstborn of Joseph and was born in Egypt.)

2) Bristleworm (Joel 1:4).

3) Sabbath's day (Acts 1:12).

4) Forty (1 Chronicles 29:26 – 27).

5) Patmos (Revelation 1:9 – 12).

6) Two hundred (2 Samuel 14:23 – 26).

Score Correct _____ Date _____ Name _____
Study Notes: _____
_____

Quiz 142

1) Is the book of Kislon in the Old Testament, the New Testament, or neither?
2) In Revelation 6, what is the name of the fourth horseman?
   Death, power, brimstone, terror
3) Who was the son of Gera, a Benjamite, and a man lefthanded?
   Ludim, Ehud, Ashbel, Paulus
4) What minor prophet described clouds as the dust of the Lord's feet?
   Habakkuk, Zephaniah, Haggai, Nahum
5) As mentioned in six verses, what was "Iconium"?
   Metal for shields, city, mountain range, fiery idol
6) The five daughters of Zelophehad included Mahlah, Hoglah, Milcah, Tirzah, and _____?
   Damaris, Asenath, Gomer, Noah

ANSWERS:
1) Neither. (Kislon was a prince of Benjamin and the father of Elidad.)
2) Death (Revelation 6:7 – 8).
3) Ehud (Judges 3:15).
4) Nahum (Nahum 1:3).
5) City (Acts 13:51; 14:1, 19, 21; 16:2, 2 Timothy 3:11).
6) Noah (obviously not the one of ark fame; Joshua 17:3).

Score Correct_____ Date_____ Name _____
Study Notes: _____
_____

Quiz 143

1) Is the book of Fortunatus in the Old Testament, the New Testament, or neither?

2) The Gileadites tested others to see if they were their enemies (Ephraimites) by making them say what word correctly?
Selah, Shibboleth, Samuel, Smyrna

3) Who said his wife thought he had strange (bad) breath?
Ananias, Keturah, Zebedee, Job

4) What was the relationship of David, the most prominent king of Israel, to Ruth?
Son, brother, grandson, great-grandson

5) As described in scripture, what type of man was Elymas?
Warrior, sorcerer, Greek, leprous

6) Manna was white, tasted like wafers made with honey, and was like what kind of seed?
Royal, coriander, gourd, barley

ANSWERS:

1) Neither. (Fortunatus was one of the more spiritual believers in the Corinthian Church.)

2) Shibboleth (Judges 12:4 – 6).

3) Job (Job 19:17).

4) Great-grandson (Ruth 4: 13 – 17).

5) Sorcerer (Acts 13:8).

6) Coriander (Exodus 16:31).

Score Correct_____ Date_____ Name _____
*Study Notes:*_____
_____

Quiz 144

1) Is the book of Genesis in the Old Testament, the New Testament, or neither?

2) After Jonah was in the belly of the great fish for three days and nights, why did the fish vomit him out upon the dry land? Sailors harpooned it, the fish became irritated, Jonah convinced it, the Lord spoke to the fish

3) What do the seven stars represent in Revelation 1? Continents, angels, seas, beasts

4) In the book of Habakkuk, who is referred to as "that bitter and hasty nation"? Syrians, Chaldeans, Egyptians, Persians

5) Jesus said, "That whosoever believeth in me should not abide in _____"? Fear, darkness, shame, sin

6) The shortest book in the Old Testament is the book of Obadiah, which prophesied about what kingdom's doom? Greece, Edom, Bashan, Persia

ANSWERS:

1) Old Testament. (Genesis is the first book of the Old Testament, thus also the first book of the Bible.)

2) The Lord spoke to the fish (Jonah 1:17, 2: 10).

3) Angels (Revelation 1:20).

4) Chaldeans (Habakkuk 1:6 – 7).

5) Darkness (John 12:46).

6) Edom (Obadiah 1:1).

Score Correct _____ Date _____ Name _____

Study Notes: _____

_____

Quiz 145

1) Is the book of 3 John in the Old Testament, the New Testament, or neither?

2) After Jehoiada's death, what did king Joash of Judah do to Zechariah, Jehoiada's son?
Made him king, exiled him, had him stoned to death, honored him with a banquet

3) From the book of Ecclesiastes, there is "a time to mourn and a time to _____"?
Leave, dance, love, profit

4) Upon which mount does Obadiah say there shall be deliverance for the Lord's people?
Moriah, Zion, Abarim, Ebal

5) Where was Samson imprisoned after being betrayed by Delilah?
Bethany, Antioch, Gaza, Damascus

6) In the book of John, what cannot one tell from where it comes nor goes?
Serpent, lust, wind, war

ANSWERS:

1) New Testament. (3 John is the twenty-fifth book of the New Testament.)

2) Had him stoned to death (2 Chronicles 24:17 – 22).

3) Dance (Ecclesiastes 3:4).

4) Zion (Obadiah 1:17).

5) Gaza (Judges 16:1 – 3, 21).

6) Wind (John 3:8).

Score Correct_____ Date_____ Name _____
Study Notes: _____
_____

The Prophet Jeremiah

Quiz 146

1) Is the book of Horeb in the Old Testament, the New Testament, or neither?

2) From the laws of ancient Israel if a man had a stubborn and rebellious son who would not obey, the men of his city shalt do what to the son?
Beat, stone, drown, exile

3) Though they join forces, who will not go unpunished?
Heathens, mortals, beasts, the wicked

4) Who was God talking to when he said, "The voice of thy brother's blood crieth unto me from the ground."?
Andrew, Jacob, Aaron, Cain

5) From 1 Peter, what types of stones were built into a spiritual house?
Lively, rolling, precious, river

6) In addition to being a frequent companion of Paul, what was Luke's profession?
Scholar, knight, physician, king

ANSWERS:
1) Neither. (Mount Horeb was the scene of the burning bush.)
2) Stone (Deuteronomy 21:18 – 21).
3) The wicked (Proverbs 11:21).
4) Cain (referring to Abel's murder; Genesis 4:9 – 10).
5) Lively (1 Peter 2:5).
6) Physician (Colossians 4:14).

Score Correct_____ Date_____ Name _____
Study Notes:_____
_____

Quiz 147

1) Is the book of Olympas in the Old Testament, the New Testament, or neither?

2) In 1 and 2 Chronicles, which king of Assyria is mentioned in addition to Pul?
Tilgathpilneser, Thahash, Zadok, Zaphnathpaaneah

3) As some disciples were known by more than one name, what was Saul also called?
Paul, David, Sisera, Solomon

4) What did the chief priests purchase with the blood money they got back from a remorseful Judas Iscariot?
Two oxen, a potter's field, a copper chalice, barley grain

5) In 2 Corinthians, what disaster did Paul experience three times?
Forsakenness, shipwreck, earthquake, stabbing

6) Whose vision encompassed a brass appearance of a man with a line of flax in his hand and a measuring rod at the gateway of a building on a very high mountain?
Eliphaz, Abraham, Ezekiel, Micaiah

ANSWERS:

1) Neither. (Olympas was a believer at Rome of which Paul sent a salutation.)

2) Tilgathpilneser (1 Chronicles 5:6, 2 Chronicles 28:20).

3) Paul (Acts 13:9).

4) A potter's field (Matthew 27:3 – 7).

5) Shipwreck (2 Corinthians 11:25).

6) Ezekiel (Ezekiel 40:2 – 6).

Score Correct _____ Date _____ Name _____

Study Notes: _____

_____

Quiz 148

1) Is the book of Nebuchadnezzar in the Old Testament, the New Testament, or neither?

2) In Paul's word to the Ephesians, what kind of church should be presented to Christ; one that should be holy and without _____?

   Fault, hypocrites, blemish, hesitation

3) Who or what was Beersheba in the Bible?

   The wife of David, a city, Deborah's sister, a mountain

4) After Jesus calmed the storm of wind on the lake and the raging water, what did he accuse the disciples of lacking?

   Courage, faith, strength, wisdom

5) In Exodus, who murdered an Egyptian and hid him in the sand?

   Adam, Reuben, Moses, Jacob

6) Who was the handmaiden of Leah that became the mother of two of the twelve tribes of Israel?

   Hagar, Bilhah, Esther, Zilpah

ANSWERS:

1) Neither. (Nebuchadnezzar was the king of Babylon and the first Gentile monarch.)

2) Blemish (Ephesians 5:27).

3) A city (Genesis 26:33).

4) Faith (Luke 8:23 – 25).

5) Moses (Exodus 2:11 – 12).

6) Zilpah (the mother of Asher and Gad; Genesis 30:11 – 13; 35:22 – 26).

Score Correct_____ Date_____ Name _____

*Study Notes:*_____

_____

Quiz 149

1) Is the book of Philippi in the Old Testament, the New Testament, or neither?

2) According to Isaiah, those that wait upon the Lord shall renew their strength; they shall run and not be _____?
Slow, weary, forsaken, deceived

3) In Genesis, who found grace in the eyes of the Lord?
Noah, Moses, Adam, Eve

4) What prophet did God tell to take a sharp knife and barber's razor and shave his head and beard?
Ezekiel, Gad, Iddo, Manahen

5) How old was Isaac when he took Rebekah as his wife?
14, 40, 80, 130

6) How shall Christ send his angels to gather the redeemed when he returns to earth; with a great sound of _____?
A trumpet, thunder, stampeding horses, mighty wind

ANSWERS:

1) Neither. (Philippi was the chief city of eastern Macedonia with the present municipality, Filippoi, located near its ruins.)

2) Weary (Isaiah 40:31).

3) Noah (Genesis 6:8).

4) Ezekiel (Ezekiel 5:1).

5) 40 (Genesis 25:20).

6) A trumpet (Matthew 24:30 – 31).

Score Correct _____ Date _____ Name _____

Study Notes: _____

_____

Quiz 150

1) Is the book of Nisroch in the Old Testament, the New Testament, or neither?

2) From the book of Ecclesiastes, there is "a time to weep and a time to _____"?
   Laugh, hate, speak, lose

3) Who was the steward that managed the household of Herod (Antipas)?
   Bani, Chuza, Kore, Arza

4) Satan's chained sentence will last how many years?
   One hundred, five hundred, one thousand, five thousand

5) Who tried to walk on water but was terrified and began to sink?
   Paul, Mark, Peter, Thomas

6) Barabbas, who was released before Jesus, was previously sentenced to death as a _____?
   Blasphemer, murderer, fornicator, robber

ANSWERS:
1) Neither. (Nisroch was an Assyrian god.)
2) Laugh (Ecclesiastes 3:4).
3) Chuza (Luke 8:3).
4) One thousand (Revelation 20:1 – 2).
5) Peter (Matthew 14:25 – 30).
6) Robber (John 18:40).

Score Correct_____ Date_____ Name _____
Study Notes:_____
_____

Quiz 151

1) Is the book of Nadab in the Old Testament, the New Testament, or neither?

2) What king tore his clothes after hearing the news of the finding of the Book of Law in the temple?
Menaham, Hoshea, Josiah, Shallum

3) In Proverbs, which waters are sweet?
Free, stolen, still, deep

4) When the Lord spoke to Moses about the Sabbath, he said it is a sign throughout _____?
The beloved, generations, the lands, deliverances

5) Who was a mighty man of valor but the son of a harlot?
Jeroboam, Eliada, Jephthah, Adnah

6) In the Sermon on the Mount in Matthew 5, where do we never put our light?
Under a bushel, atop a tree, around the house, below the water

ANSWERS:
1) Neither. (Nadab was the elder son of Aaron.)
2) Josiah (2 Kings 22:3, 8 – 11).
3) Stolen (Proverbs 9:17).
4) Generations (Exodus 31:12 – 13).
5) Jephthah (Judges 11:1).
6) Under a bushel (Matthew 5:14 – 15).

Score Correct _____ Date _____ Name _____
Study Notes: _____
_____

Quiz 152

1) Is the book of Vestry in the Old Testament, the New Testament, or neither?

2) Whose fame and wisdom included his knowledge of beasts, birds, reptiles, and fish?
Samuel, Solomon, Samson, Saul

3) What will a faithful man abound with?
Friends, blessings, life, love

4) When he died, whose eyes were not dim, nor his natural vigor diminished?
Moses, David, Paul, Daniel

5) In Psalm 114, what did the mountains skip like?
Rams, lambs, waves, children

6) What leper king was buried in a field after which his son, Jotham, reigned?
Jehoram, Uzziah, Ahaziah, Pekah

ANSWERS:

1) Neither. (Vestry has the meaning of wardrobe in the Bible.)
2) Solomon (1 Kings 4:30 – 33).
3) Blessings (Proverbs 28:20).
4) Moses (Deuteronomy 34:7).
5) Rams (Psalm 114:4).
6) Uzziah (2 Chronicles 26:23).

Score Correct_____ Date_____ Name _____
Study Notes:_____

Quiz 153

1) Is the book of Aaron in the Old Testament, the New Testament, or neither?

2) What same word goes in both blanks from a verse in Matthew 6, "But if ye forgive not men their _____, neither will your Father forgive your _____."?
   Shortcomings, greed, trespasses, vengeance

3) When we ask God for wisdom, it must be without _____?
   Fear, wavering, hope, righteousness

4) In the book of Hebrews, what is the substance of things hoped for, the evidence of things not seen?
   Repentance, faith, redemption, windfalls

5) Michal, who was David's first wife, was later given to whom by king Saul?
   Belteshazzar, Phalti, Aridatha, Shedeur

6) When the reincarnated Jesus came into the coasts of Caesarea Philippi, he was mistaken for all of the following except _____?
   David, John the Baptist, Elias, Jeremias

ANSWERS:

1) Neither. (Aaron was the name of the brother of Moses.)
2) Trespasses (Matthew 6:15).
3) Wavering (James 1:5 – 6).
4) Faith (Hebrews 11:1).
5) Phalti (the son of Laish; 1 Samuel 25:44).
6) David (Matthew 16:13 – 14).

Score Correct _____ Date_____ Name _____
Study Notes: _____
_____

Quiz 154

1) Is the book of Nob in the Old Testament, the New Testament, or neither?

2) Who said, "The hour is coming, and now is, when the dead shall hear the voice of the Son of God"?
Jesus, John the Baptist, Peter, Matthias

3) In the book of Revelation, what was the name of the old serpent?
The Devil, Aster, Nehushtan, Lucifer

4) Joseph was sold into slavery to the Ishmeelites for how many pieces of silver and taken to Egypt?
Ten, twenty, thirty, fifty

5) What was an abomination unto the Egyptians?
The coppersmith, idol worshippers, every shepherd, false prophets

6) Which book begins, "Now king David was old and stricken in years; and they covered him with clothes, but he gat no heat."?
Numbers, 1 Kings, Psalms, Joel

ANSWERS:
1) Neither. (Nob was a city of priests in the tribe of Benjamin near Jerusalem.)
2) Jesus (John 5:25).
3) The Devil (Revelation 12:9).
4) Twenty (Genesis 37:28).
5) Every shepherd (Genesis 46:34).
6) 1 Kings (1 Kings 1:1).

Score Correct _____ Date_____ Name _____
Study Notes: _____
_____

Quiz 155

1) Is the book of Revelation in the Old Testament, the New Testament, or neither?

2) Fill in the blank from Romans 3: "For all have sinned, and come short of the _____ of God."
Will, glory, peace, voice

3) Who was the king of Salem and priest said to have neither mother nor father?
Solomon, David, Melchisedec, Sargon

4) How many of Pharaoh's Egyptian army escaped the returning waters of the Red Sea?
Zero, one, ten, one hundred

5) What priest had two sons, Hophni and Phinehas, who were evil and killed in battle?
Eli, Abiathar, Bukki, Eleazar

6) Who became leprous for questioning whether the Lord had only spoken through Moses and not through others, too?
Miriam, Rachel, Syntyche, Judith

ANSWERS:

1) New Testament. (Revelation is the twenty-seventh and final book of the New Testament and Bible.)

2) Glory (Romans 3:23).

3) Melchisedec (Hebrews 7:1 – 3).

4) Zero (Exodus 14:26 – 28).

5) Eli (1 Samuel 1:3, 4:11, 17).

6) Miriam (Numbers 12:1 – 2, 10).

Score Correct _____ Date _____ Name _____

Study Notes: _____

_____

Quiz 156

1) Is the book of Nahor in the Old Testament, the New Testament, or neither?

2) Jesus said, "For where your treasure is, there will your _____ be also."
   Toils, heart, sanctum, church

3) In John, who was a Pharisee and ruler among the Jews?
   Zacchaeus, Nicodemus, Judas, Peter

4) After being captured, what king's thumbs and great toes were cut off, for he had done the same to seventy (kings) previous?
   Jehu, Adonibezek, Josiah, Herod

5) How many beasts rising out of the sea did Daniel have a dream about?
   Four, seven, thirteen, twenty

6) At the time of the singing birds in Song of Solomon, whose voice was heard in the land?
   Trumpet, tempest, truth, turtle

ANSWERS:

1) Neither. (Nahor a son of Serug and grandfather of Abraham.)

2) Heart (Matthew 6:21; Luke 12:34).

3) Nicodemus (John 3:1).

4) Adonibezek (Judges 1:6 – 7).

5) Four (Daniel 7:1 – 3).

6) Turtle (meaning turtledove; Song of Solomon 2:12).

Score Correct_____ Date_____ Name _____

Study Notes:_____

Quiz 157

1) Is the book of 3 Peter in the Old Testament, the New Testament, or neither?

2) Who confronted David about his sin concerning the death of Uriah the Hittite and taking his wife, Bathsheba?
   Abdeel, Hadlai, Jozadak, Nathan

3) What king wanted to see miracles when the arrested Jesus was before him?
   Pilate, Shishak, Herod, Solomon

4) From Proverbs: "Be not wise in thine own _____; fear the Lord, and depart from evil."
   Eyes, flock, thoughts, journey

5) Which book ends, "And Obed begat Jesse, and Jesse begat David."?
   Esther, Joshua, Ruth, Jonah

6) Who was the only man in the Bible to have the Lord as his undertaker?
   Lazarus, Moses, Noah, Jesse

ANSWERS:

1) Neither. (3 Peter is fictitious, but 1 and 2 Peter are the twenty-first and twenty-second books of the New Testament.)

2) Nathan (2 Samuel 12:9, 13, 24).

3) Herod (Luke 23:7 – 8).

4) Eyes (Proverbs 3:7).

5) Ruth (Ruth 4:22).

6) Moses (Deuteronomy 34:5 – 6).

Score Correct _____ Date _____ Name _____

Study Notes: _____

_____

Quiz 158

1) Is the book of Eglon in the Old Testament, the New Testament, or neither?

2) The Lord caused the sundial's shadow to go back how many degrees, as a signal to Hezekiah that he would have a longer life?
Ten, twenty-five, fifty, one hundred

3) Lemuel warns kings to avoid what, lest they forget the law and pervert justice?
Concubines, wine, darkness, warfare

4) When the soldiers crucified Jesus, what did they do with his coat?
Cut it in ribbons, gave it to a child, cast lots for it, burned it

5) Which book ends, "Little children, keep yourselves from idols. Amen."?
1 John, Jude, Mark, Amos

6) What Jewish feast and celebration commemorates God's deliverance of the Jewish people through Esther?
Purim, Yom Kippur, Pesach, Matzah

ANSWERS:

1) Neither. (Eglon was a king of Moab who was slain by Ehud.)
2) Ten (2 Kings 20:8 – 11).
3) Wine (Proverbs 31:4 – 5).
4) Cast lots for it (John 19:23–24).
5) 1 John (1 John 5:21).
6) Purim (Esther 9:22 – 26).

Score Correct_____ Date_____ Name _____

Study Notes:_____

_____

Quiz 159

1) Is the book of Ehud in the Old Testament, the New Testament, or neither?
2) Fill in the blank from Ephesians: "A man leave his father and mother, and shall be joined unto his wife, and they two shall be _____."
   Married jointly, one flesh, forever one, heaven sent
3) Which book of these comes before the others in the Bible's Old Testament?
   Hosea, Job, Ruth, Jeremiah
4) What word did Jesus pronounce on the Pharisees eight times in one speech?
   Misery, gloom, murk, woe
5) In biblical times, what did "sup" mean?
   Journey, pray, dine, wash
6) What parts of the New Jerusalem's city walls were garnished with all manner of precious stones?
   Sides, foundations, fronts, tops

ANSWERS:
1) Neither. (Ehud was a left-handed man and a ruler in Israel.)
2) One flesh (Ephesians 5:31).
3) Ruth (Hosea is the twenty-eighth book, Job the eighteenth, Ruth the eighth, Jeremiah the twenty-fourth).
4) Woe (Matthew 23:13 – 29).
5) Dine (Revelation 3:20).
6) Foundations (Revelation 21:19 – 20).

Score Correct _____ Date _____ Name _____

Study Notes: _____

_____

Quiz 160

1) Is the book of Jonah in the Old Testament, the New Testament, or neither?

2) Along with his sons, who was the first to be cremated in the Bible?

   Samuel, Solomon, Shadrach, Saul

3) Who or what drove Jesus into the wilderness to be tempted?

   The Devil, wild beasts, the Holy Spirit, Mary and Martha

4) In Proverbs, what stones are worth less than either wisdom or a good wife?

   Rubies, river, minas, emeralds

5) Where is the story of Samson and Delilah found?

   Joshua 22, Judges 16, Job 3, Amos 34

6) Both John the Baptist and Jesus were circumcised at the age of how many days?

   Three, eight, fourteen, seventeen

ANSWERS:

1) Old Testament. (Jonah is the thirty-second book of the Old Testament.)

2) Saul (1 Samuel 31:12).

3) The Holy Spirit (Mark 1:11 – 13).

4) Rubies (Proverbs 8:11, 31:10).

5) Judges 16 (Judges 16:1 – 31).

6) Eight (Luke 1:59, 2:21).

Score Correct _____ Date _____ Name _____

Study Notes: _____

_____

Quiz 161

1) Is the book of Hezekiah in the Old Testament, the New Testament, or neither?

2) To whom did Jesus say, "I am the resurrection and the life: he that believeth in me, though he were dead, yet shall he live."?
   His disciples, Mary, Martha, Dorcas

3) What soldier murdered Amasa while taking him by the beard to kiss him?
   Abishai, Joab, Sheba, Bichri

4) Who bet thirty men thirty sheets (linen wraps) and thirty changes of clothes (garments) they could not solve his riddle?
   Moses, Samson, Daniel, Paul

5) In Revelation, Jesus tells us to be zealous and to do what?
   Repent, share, love, witness

6) What did Amos prophesy would happen to the city of Gilgal?
   Go into captivity, come to naught, brought unto fire, smitten by the sword

ANSWERS:

1) Neither. (Hezekiah was the son and successor of Ahaz as king of Judah.)

2) Martha (John 11:24 – 25).

3) Joab (2 Samuel 20:8 – 10).

4) Samson (Judges 14:12 – 14).

5) Repent (Revelation 3:19).

6) Go into captivity (Amos 5:5).

Score Correct _____ Date _____ Name _____

Study Notes: _____

_____

Quiz 162

1) Is the book of Jericho in the Old Testament, the New Testament, or neither?

2) Who boasted to his two wives, Adah and Zillah, that he had killed a young man?
   Baanah, Herod, Lamech, Jehu

3) How many others were crucified along with Jesus?
   None, one, two, three

4) In the book of Revelation, what stone resembles the rainbow circling God's throne in heaven?
   Emerald, ruby, pearl, sapphire

5) Who was the father of Isaac?
   Aaron, Noah, Abraham, Peter

6) In Jarius' household, who was sick to the point of death of a blood disease?
   His sister, his daughter, his mother, his wife

ANSWERS:

1) Neither. (Jericho was a fenced city famed for its walls falling after Joshua's Israelite army marched around it blowing their trumpets.)

2) Lamech (Genesis 4:23).

3) Two (John 19:18; Mark 15:27).

4) Emerald (Revelation 4:1 – 3).

5) Abraham (Genesis 21:3).

6) His daughter (Mark 5:22 – 25).

Score Correct_____ Date_____ Name _____

Study Notes:_____

_____

Quiz 163

1) Is the book of Judith in the Old Testament, the New Testament, or neither?

2) What were the children of Israel to wear upon the borders of their garments throughout generations, as reminders to obey the commandments of the Lord?
Ribband of blue, lace of yellow, splice of red, silver glitter

3) Who died after accidentally touching the Ark of the Covenant?
Achan, Zedekiah, Naboth, Uzzah

4) Samuel, who was the last of the judges of Israel, traveled on a circuit that did not include which of these cities?
Bethel, Calah, Gilgal, Mizpeh

5) At what Philistine city did Samson slay thirty men?
Ashdod, Ai, Achaia, Ashkelon

6) After Jesus' crucifixion who were responsible for preparing his body for burial?
Mary and Martha, Joseph of Arimathaea and Nicodemus, Thomas and Peter, Nathanael and Pilate

ANSWERS:

1) Neither. (Judith was one of the two Hittite wives of Esau.)
2) Ribband of blue (Numbers 15:38 – 39).
3) Uzzah (2 Samuel 6:3 – 11).
4) Calah (1 Samuel 7: 15 – 16).
5) Ashkelon (Judges 14:19 – 20).
6) Joseph of Arimathaea and Nicodemus (John 19:38 – 40).

Score Correct _____ Date_____ Name _____

Study Notes: _____

_____

Quiz 164

1) Is the book of Exodus in the Old Testament, the New Testament, or neither?

2) What was the problem of the daughter whose mother was a Greek, a Syrophenician by nation?
Wearing man's garment, adulterous, had an unclean spirit, idolater

3) Where did Paul go to prepare to preach the gospel?
Jerusalem, Syria, Greece, Arabia

4) About how many swine ran violently into the sea after Jesus drove the legion of devils into them?
Two, twenty, two hundred, two thousand

5) According to James, the effectual fervent prayer of what type man availeth much?
Patient, holy, righteous, elderly

6) Where did Jesus miraculously resurrect the only son of a widow during a burial ceremony?
Megiddo, Nain, Lachish, Joppa

ANSWERS:

1) Old Testament (Exodus is the second book of the Old Testament.)
2) Had an unclean spirit (Mark 7:25 – 26).
3) Arabia (Galatians 1:1, 17).
4) Two thousand (Mark 5:1, 8 – 13).
5) Righteous (James 5:16).
6) Nain (Luke 7:11 – 15).

Score Correct_____ Date_____ Name _____
Study Notes:_____
_____

The Prophet Amos

Quiz 165

1) Is the book of Hebron in the Old Testament, the New Testament, or neither?

2) When Jesus fed the five thousand, in what sized groups did the people sit down upon the green grass to eat?
Pairs, fours, tens, fifties and hundreds

3) According to Colossians, what do we have through Jesus' blood?
Love, eternity, hope, redemption

4) After Peter was angelically released from prison, who answered when he went to the house of Mary?
Huldah, Rhoda, Persis, Noadiah

5) Which of these biblical prophets was descended from a king?
Asaph, Zephaniah, Hanani, Shemaiah

6) How did God identify himself when speaking from the burning bush?
I AM THAT I AM, KING OF ALL, JESUS CHRIST, LORD OF JEHOVA

ANSWERS:

1) Neither. (Hebron was king David's first capital city of Judah.)
2) Fifties and hundreds (Mark 6:39 – 44).
3) Redemption (Colossians 1:13 – 14).
4) Rhoda (Acts 12:7 – 13).
5) Zephaniah (Zephaniah 1:1).
6) I AM THAT I AM (Exodus 3:4, 14).

Score Correct_____ Date_____ Name _____
*Study Notes:*_____
_____

Quiz 166

1) Is the book of 2 Samuel in the Old Testament, the New Testament, or neither?

2) When Jesus raised Jairus' daughter from the dead, what did he say that was interpreted as, "Damsel, I say unto thee, arise."?
   Codex sinaiticus, Lama sabachthani, Talitha cumi, Ephpha-tha selah

3) Who burned David's city of Ziklag with fire?
   Amalekites, Nazarites, Gibeonites, Israelites

4) How long did Jesus say the Son of man would be in the heart of the earth?
   Overnight, three days and three nights, sunrise to sunset, seven days and seven nights

5) What sort of men shall suck the poison of asps (snakes)?
   Wicked, aged, tribal, leper

6) Who judged Israel twenty and two years, had thirty sons, and was buried in Camon?
   Samson, Jair, Ephraim, Gideon

ANSWERS:

1) Old Testament. (2 Samuel is the tenth book of the Old Testament.)

2) Talitha cumi (Mark 5:22 – 23, 41).

3) Amalekites (1 Samuel 30:1).

4) Three days and three nights (Matthew 12:40).

5) Wicked (Job 20:12 – 16).

6) Jair (Judges 10:3 – 5).

Score Correct _____ Date _____ Name _____

Study Notes: _____

_____

Quiz 167

1) Is the book of 3 Timothy in the Old Testament, the New Testament, or neither?

2) When Jesus cleared the temple of merchants, he said to the ones that sold doves, "Take these things hence; make not my Father's house an house of _____."
Trade, merchandise, money-changers, thieves

3) How many sons did Judah have?
Three, five, six, twelve

4) According to Paul in the book of Galatians, in what country is Mount Sinai?
Arabia, Syria, Lebanon, Egypt

5) Samuel, last of the judges of Israel, was followed by whom as king?
Rehoboam, Saul, David, Zimri

6) Who was Israel's shortest-reigning king, serving only seven days, because of his murderous ways?
Shalmaneser, Zimri, So, Menahem

ANSWERS:

1) Neither. (3 Timothy is fictitious, but 1 and 2 Timothy are the fifteenth and sixteenth books of the New Testament.)
2) Merchandise (John 2:13 – 16).
3) Five (Er, Onan, Shelah, Pharez, and Zerah; Genesis 46:12).
4) Arabia (Galatians 4:25).
5) Saul (1 Samuel 15:1).
6) Zimri (1 Kings 16:15 – 16).

Score Correct_____ Date_____ Name _____
Study Notes:_____
_____

Quiz 168

1) Is the book of Uzziel in the Old Testament, the New Testament, or neither?

2) In Proverbs, what type of person turns on his bed like a door upon its hinges, and hideth his hand in his bosom?
   Childish, slothful, elderly, vengeful

3) Who told Saul that rebellion was as bad as witchcraft?
   Moloch, Mamath, Marduk, Samuel

4) After Jesus went out to a mountainside, how long did he pray before choosing his twelve disciples?
   All night, two days, seven days, forty days

5) How many times was Naaman dipped into the Jordan River to be healed of leprosy?
   One, two, four, seven

6) Who spake against Moses because of the Ethiopian woman whom he had married?
   Amram and Jochebed, Miriam and Aaron, Samson and Delilah, Hagar and Gomer

ANSWERS:

1) Neither. (There are a half dozen men bearing the name Uzziel. Tribal family members are spoken of as Uzzielites.)

2) Slothful (Proverbs 26:13 – 15).

3) Samuel (1 Samuel 15:22 – 25).

4) All night (Luke 6:12 – 13).

5) Seven (2 Kings 5:14 – 17).

6) Miriam and Aaron (Numbers 12:1).

Score Correct_____ Date_____ Name _____
Study Notes: _____
_____

Quiz 169

1) Is the book of Henika in the Old Testament, the New Testament, or neither?

2) Fill in the blank from Psalm 51: "Create in me a clean _____, O God; and renew a right spirit within me."
   Life, understanding, fulfillment, heart

3) Whose daughter had the twelve-lettered name of Kerenhappuch?
   Potiphar, Zimri, Goliath, Job

4) Of these books, which comes before the others in the New Testament?
   Titus, Jude, Colossians, Galatians

5) Jesus said in John, "I am the good _____."
   Samaritan, storyteller, fisherman, shepherd

6) After being banished, which king let his hair grow as long as eagles' feathers and his nails like birds' claws?
   Solomon, Herod, Asa, Nebuchadnezzar

ANSWERS:

1) Neither. (Henika is an old word from Greek texts meaning "at which time.")

2) Heart (Psalm 51:10).

3) Job (Job 42:14).

4) Galatians. (Titus is the seventeenth New Testament book, Jude is the twenty-sixth, Colossians the twelfth, and Galatians the ninth.)

5) Shepherd (John 10:14).

6) Nebuchadnezzar (Daniel 4:33).

Score Correct_____ Date_____ Name _____

Study Notes:_____

_____

Quiz 170

1) Is the book of Hosea in the Old Testament, the New Testament, or neither?

2) Fill in the blank (using same number) from Luke 17: "And if he trespass against thee _____ times in a day, and _____ times in a day turn again to thee, saying, I repent; thou shalt forgive him."?
   Two, three, seven, twelve

3) Aholah, Aholibah, and Rahab were all what?
   Queens, prostitutes, priests, vineyards

4) Who played and danced in a linen ephod when the Ark of the Covenant was being brought into Jerusalem?
   Rehoboam, Abijah, David, Yachin

5) What position of authority did Pontius Pilate hold?
   Centurion, governor, saint, pharaoh

6) Flagons are mentioned five times in the Bible and associated with _____?
   Water, wine, spears, camels

ANSWERS:

1) Old Testament. (Hosea is the twenty-eighth book of the Old Testament.)

2) Seven (Luke 17:4).

3) Prostitutes (Ezekiel 23:5, 11; Joshua 2:1).

4) David (1 Chronicles 15:27 – 29).

5) Governor (Luke 3:1).

6) Wine (2 Samuel 6:19, 1 Chronicles 16:3, Song of Solomon 2:5, Isaiah 22:24, Hosea 3:1).

Score Correct _____ Date _____ Name _____

Study Notes: _____

_____

Quiz 171

1) Is the book of Isaiah in the Old Testament, the New Testament, or neither?
2) During Solomon's reign, there was so much wealth in Israel that what was as common as stones in Jerusalem?
   Bread, myrrh, cedar, silver
3) In the new creation, the wolf shall feed with the _____?
   Children, fishes, lamb, ox
4) A proud look, a lying tongue, and hands that shed innocent blood are among the things hated by whom in Proverbs?
   John the Baptist, Isaiah, Solomon, the Lord
5) How many books of the Bible begin with the letter "G"?
   One, two, three, four
6) After Jesus was questioned by the high priest, with what did an officer strike him when he thought Jesus had improperly responded?
   Snap of a whip, palm of his hand, swift kick, elbow to stomach

ANSWERS:
1) Old Testament. (Isaiah is the twenty-third book of the Old Testament.)
2) Silver (1 Kings 10:25 – 27).
3) Lamb (Isaiah 65:17, 25).
4) The Lord (Proverbs 6:16 – 17).
5) Two. (Genesis the first book of the Old Testament and Galatians the ninth book of the New Testament.)
6) Palm of his hand (John 18:19 – 22).

Score Correct _____ Date _____ Name _____

Study Notes: _____

_____

Quiz 172

1) Is the book of Igdaliah in the Old Testament, the New Testament, or neither?

2) Who was the son of king Baladan of Babylon who sent letters and a present when king Hezekiah of Judah recovered from his illness?

   Nephthalim, Merodachbaladan, Parshandatha, Shephuphan

3) In the book of James, he that wavereth (doubts) is like a _____?

   Limb in the wind, wandering sheep, wave of the sea, lost child

4) Which of these men in the Bible is mentioned only once?

   Jeush, Narcissus, Ziha, Jonadab

5) What did Noah begin "to be" after the flood?

   Husbandman, shepherd, carpenter, teacher

6) In the book of Ecclesiastes, Solomon said that every man should eat and drink, and enjoy the good of all his labour, for it is the _____ of God.

   Will, joy, gift, strength

ANSWERS:

1) Neither. (Igdaliah was the father of Hanan and had a chamber in the Temple.)

2) Merodachbaladan (Isaiah 39:1).

3) Wave of the sea (James 1:6).

4) Narcissus (Romans 16:11).

5) Husbandman (Genesis 9:20).

6) Gift (Ecclesiastes 3:13).

Score Correct _____ Date _____ Name _____

Study Notes: _____

Quiz 173

1) Is the book of 3 Kings in the Old Testament, the New Testament, or neither?
2) Where did the people make Saul the king after he had led them to victory over the Ammonites?
   Sidon, Penuel, Gilgal, Nain
3) When Jesus was born in Bethlehem, who was the king of Judea?
   Pontius Pilate, Herod, Tiberius Caesar, Solomon
4) What did God provide as a substitute for Abraham who was about to sacrifice his son Isaac?
   Horse, ram, cow, raven
5) Who wrote a letter to Felix concerning Paul?
   King Darius, John, Claudius Lysias, Peter
6) In a parable, those who hear his sayings and obey them built their house upon _____?
   A rock, the sand, a stream, the shore

ANSWERS:
1) Neither. (3 Kings is fictitious, but 1 Kings and 2 Kings are the eleventh and twelfth books of the Old Testament.)
2) Gilgal (1 Samuel 11:11 – 15).
3) Herod (Matthew 2:1).
4) Ram (Genesis 22:9 – 13).
5) Claudius Lysias (Acts 23:24 – 26).
6) A rock (Matthew 7:24).

Score Correct_____ Date_____ Name _____
Study Notes:_____
_____

Quiz 174

1) Is the book of Jude in the Old Testament, the New Testament, or neither?

2) In the parable of the rich man and a beggar named Lazarus, where did the beggar go when he died?
Abraham's bosom, rich rewards, table of gold, pearly gates

3) Who is referred to as the "Tishbite" in six of the Bible's verses?
Elijah, Goliath, Job, Samson

4) What kind of fire does Malachi say the Lord will be like in the day of his coming?
Goldsmith's, refiner's, furnace's, manifestation's

5) Who came and ministered unto Jesus when the devil left after tempting him?
Holy Spirit, angels, Esaias, Andrew

6) What Old Testament person was buried in a "coffin," marking the only time the word is mentioned in the entire Bible?
Adam, Noah, Moses, Joseph

ANSWERS:

1) New Testament. (Jude is the twenty-sixth book of the New Testament.)

2) Abraham's bosom. (Luke 16:19 – 23. Note: most theologians agree this was not the same Lazarus as the one raised from the dead.)

3) Elijah (1 Kings 17:1, 21:17, 28; 2 Kings 1:3, 8; 2 Kings 9:36).

4) Refiner's (Malachi 3:1 – 2).

5) Angels (Matthew 4:8 – 11).

6) Joseph (Genesis 50:26).

Score Correct _____ Date _____ Name _____
Study Notes: _____

_____

Quiz 175

1) Is the book of Job in the Old Testament, the New Testament, or neither?
2) Which son of David had been drinking much wine when he was killed by the servants of Absalom?
   Amnon, Daniel, Nathan, Solomon
3) A verse in 1 Peter compares Satan to what animal that walketh about?
   The Serpent, a roaring lion, a beheaded calf, an horse
4) How long had the four thousand been with nothing to eat in the wilderness before Jesus had compassion to feed them?
   Seven hours, two days, three days, seven days
5) Who was the father of Aaron and Moses?
   Chemosh, Jacob, Amram, Marduk
6) What moved upon the face of the waters the first day of creation?
   Glory of God, Angel of God, Son of God, Spirit of God

ANSWERS:

1) Old Testament. (Job is the eighteenth book of the Old Testament.)
2) Amnon (2 Samuel 13:28 – 29).
3) A roaring lion (1 Peter 5:8).
4) Three days (Mark 8:2, 6 – 9).
5) Amram (Exodus 6:20).
6) Spirit of God (Genesis 1:2).

Score Correct_____ Date_____ Name _____
Study Notes: _____
_____

Quiz 176

1) Is the book of Joppa in the Old Testament, the New Testament, or neither?

2) In John chapter 5, who did the sick man in the pool of Bethesda expect to heal him?
   A physician, Jesus, John the Baptist, an angel

3) God sent whom into the world to not condemn it, but to save it?
   Gabriel, his Son, Gideon, Elijah

4) Who preached "baptism of repentance" for the remission of sins?
   Jesus, John the Baptist, Stephen, Paul

5) Where did Jesus raise Lazarus from the dead?
   Smyrna, Bethany, Antioch, Cana

6) In the book of Ezekiel, God compared the foolish prophets of Israel to be what in the deserts?
   Mirages, dust, winds, foxes

ANSWERS:

1) Neither. (The town of Joppa is today known as Jaffa and is about 30 miles northwest of Jerusalem.)

2) An angel (John 5:2–7).

3) His Son (John 3:17).

4) John the Baptist (Mark 1:4, Luke 3:3, Acts 13:24, 19:4).

5) Bethany (John 11:1, 43 – 44).

6) Foxes (Ezekiel 13:2 – 4).

Score Correct _____ Date _____ Name _____
Study Notes: _____
_____

Quiz 177

1) Is the book of Boaz in the Old Testament, the New Testament, or neither?

2) For what did Hosea buy for fifteen pieces of silver and one and one-half homers of barley?
Two new chariots, freedom of his adulterous wife, seven camels, release of an Egyptian slave

3) How long after Jesus' resurrection did he ascend into heaven?
Instantly, one hour, three days, forty days

4) Upon capture, whose eyes were put out by Nebuchadnezzar's orders, then chained and sent to prison in Babylon?
Zedekiah, Onesimus, Jerimoth, Hod

5) With Joseph being his favorite, how many sons did Jacob have?
Two, five, eight, twelve

6) When Jesus rode into Jerusalem on the back of a borrowed donkey's colt, what was his reaction as he beheld the city?
He wept, he smiled, he shouted, he waved

ANSWERS:
1) Neither. (Boaz became the second husband of Ruth.)
2) Freedom of his adulterous wife (Hosea 3:1 – 3).
3) Forty days (Acts 1:2 – 3).
4) Zedekiah (Jeremiah 39:5 – 7).
5) Twelve (Genesis 35:22).
6) He wept (Luke 19:35 – 41).

Score Correct _____ Date_____ Name _____
Study Notes:_____
_____

Quiz 178

1) Is the book of Nahum in the Old Testament, the New Testament, or neither?

2) Regarding slaves, a verse in Colossians states, "Masters, give unto your servants that which is just and equal; knowing that ye also have a Master in _____."
Christ, love, heaven, man

3) How did Nicodemus imply that Jesus should be judged?
Not at all, after a hearing, before witnesses, as a false prophet

4) On a ship with 257 others, who fasted for fourteen days?
Jonah, Ahab, Paul, Omri

5) In the book of Amos, what are Moloch and Chiun?
Market gates, Gods, cities by the sea, mountains

6) Who does Paul commend in Romans 16?
Priscilla, Aquila, Phebe, Mary

ANSWERS:

1) Old Testament. (Nahum is the thirty-fourth book of the Old Testament.)

2) Heaven (Colossians 4:1).

3) After a hearing (John 7:50 – 51).

4) Paul. (Acts 27:33 – 37); Note: They all fasted.)

5) Gods (Amos 5:25 – 26).

6) Phebe (Romans 16:1).

Score Correct_____ Date_____ Name _____

Study Notes: _____

_____

Quiz 179

1) Is the book of Obal in the Old Testament, the New Testament, or neither?

2) Fill in the blank from Psalm 23: "Surely goodness and _____ shall follow me all the days of my life: and I will dwell in the house of the Lord for ever."
   Love, mercy, despair, vanity

3) What did the angel who met Joshua outside Jericho tell him to remove?
   Belt, cloak, guilt, shoe

4) What nation was described as having high habitation of ones that dwellest in the clefts of the rock?
   Dumah, Edom, Lud, Cush

5) Who, along with his men, hid in caves to avoid the wrath of Saul?
   Solomon, Ezekiel, David, Job

6) To the wife of what certain man of Zorah did an angel appear, telling her she would conceive a son?
   Samson, Manoah, Josiah, Cain

ANSWERS:

1) Neither. (Obal was a son of Joktan, mentioned in the book of Genesis.)

2) Mercy (Psalm 23:6).

3) Shoe (Joshua 5:13 – 15).

4) Edom (Obadiah 1:1 – 3).

5) David (1 Samuel 24:1 – 4).

6) Manoah (Judges 13:2 – 3).

Score Correct _____ Date _____ Name _____

Study Notes: _____

_____

Quiz 180

1) Is the book of Rachel in the Old Testament, the New Testament, or neither?

2) What did Jesus refer to Judas Iscariot as, when he was addressing the twelve disciples about their grumblings about his hard teachings?

   A loner, a wicked soul, the Devil, a lost sheep

3) How many years did Noah live after the great flood?

   1, 50, 100, 350

4) Which "Caesar" ordered all the world to be taxed, causing Mary to travel to Bethlehem while expecting the baby Jesus?

   Julius, Tiberius, Claudius, Augustus

5) In biblical times, what was the cost in shekels of silver of a chariot imported from Egypt?

   Ten, fifty, two hundred, six hundred

6) Who did Paul reason (preach) to, besides Jews, on every Sabbath in the Corinth synagogue?

   Greeks, Romans, Amaleks, Canaanites

ANSWERS:

1) Neither. (Rachel was the daughter of Laban who became the second wife of her cousin Jacob.)

2) The Devil (John 6:66 – 71).

3) 350 (Genesis 9:28).

4) Augustus (Luke 2:1 – 5).

5) Six hundred (1 Kings 10:29).

6) Greeks (Acts 18:1 – 4).

Score Correct _____ Date _____ Name _____

Study Notes: _____

_____

Quiz 181

1) Is the book of Phinehas in the Old Testament, the New Testament, or neither?

2) What did Nabal do after a night of drinking when his wife, Abigail, told him that she had prevented an attack by David the day before?
Became as a stone, gathered arms and men, died instantly, fled the land

3) What does Psalm 90 set as man's normal life span?
Seventy years, eighty years, ninety-five years, one hundred years

4) Who saw an angel stand between the earth and the heaven with a drawn sword stretched out over Jerusalem?
David, Jonah, Paul, Delilah

5) What was the beggar Bartimaeus healed of in the book of Mark?
Demons, Leprosy, Blindness, Deafness

6) In addition to wisdom, what did Solomon request of the Lord as he began his reign?
Long life, conquest, great riches, understanding heart

ANSWERS:

1) Neither. (Phinehas was the grandson of Aaron.)
2) Became as a stone (had a stroke; 1 Samuel 25:35 – 37).
3) Seventy years (Psalm 90:9 – 10).
4) David (1 Chronicles 21:16).
5) Blindness (Mark 10:46 – 52).
6) Understanding heart (1 Kings 3:9 – 12, 28).

Score Correct_____ Date_____ Name _____
Study Notes:_____
_____

Peter tries to Walk On the Water

Quiz 182

1) Is the book of Patmos in the Old Testament, the New Testament, or neither?

2) In regard to the adulterous woman who was about to be stoned, Jesus said, "He that is without _____ among you, let him first cast a stone at her."
Evil, sin, love, lust

3) Who built an altar unto the Lord, calling it Jehovah-shalom?
Noah, Gideon, Jeroboam, Moses

4) Which New Testament epistle states that visiting the fatherless and widows is a mark of pure religion?
James, Jude, Peter, John

5) Who was Ruth's first husband, before Boaz became her second?
Harhur, Chilion, Mahlon, Rephael

6) What was mingled with the wine Jesus was offered on the cross, but he refused it?
Salt, myrrh, rue, cumin

ANSWERS:

1) Neither. (Patmos is a Greek island mentioned in the book of Revelation.)
2) Sin (John 8:4 – 7).
3) Gideon (Judges 6:24).
4) James (James 1:27).
5) Mahlon (Ruth 4:10 – 13).
6) Myrrh (Mark 15:22 – 24).

Score Correct_____ Date_____ Name _____
Study Notes:_____
_____

Quiz 183

1) Is the book of Rabboni in the Old Testament, the New Testament, or neither?

2) How long had the woman had a crooked back not being able to lift herself up when Jesus said, "Woman, thou art loosed from thine infirmity."?

   A fortnight, seven days and nights, one year, eighteen years

3) What Persian queen refused to display her beauty at the court of king Ahasuerus?

   Esther, Abigail, Deborah, Vashti

4) According to Jesus, whosoever humbles himself as a child is _____ in the kingdom of heaven.

   Heartfelt, loved, greatest, honored

5) In Judges 18, what Canaanite city was burned down by the men of Dan?

   Laish, Philippi, Hebron, Jericho

6) Regarding spiritual gifts, the daughters of Jerusalem said they "will make borders of gold with studs of _____"?

   Salt, silver, souls, sins

ANSWERS:

1) Neither. (Rabboni is a Jewish title of respect.)
2) Eighteen years (Luke 13:11 – 13).
3) Vashti (Esther 1:11 – 12).
4) Greatest (Matthew 18:4).
5) Laish (Judges 18:27 – 29).
6) Silver (Song of Solomon 1:5, 11).

Score Correct_____ Date_____ Name _____

Study Notes: _____

_____

Quiz 184

1) Is the book of Bath in the Old Testament, the New Testament, or neither?

2) What Israelite's goods were burned after he was stoned to death for stealing and hiding part of the spoil taken at the destruction of Jericho?
Zerah, Edom, Keilah, Achan

3) From Psalm 135, Sihon was king of the Amorites, and who was king of Bashan?
Ur, Og, Tu, Za

4) How many times is the word "trinity" mentioned in the Bible including with the phrase "holy trinity"?
Zero, one, seven, twenty-two

5) Who called on the Lord for a drink of water after he had slain a thousand men?
Elijah, Jeremiah, Samson, Ezekiel

6) Paul writes in 2 Timothy 4: "I have fought a good fight, I have finished my course, I have kept the _____."
Faith, spirit, redeemer, inspiration

ANSWERS:

1) Neither. (Bath was a liquid measure, the tenth part of a homer.)
2) Achan (Joshua 7:18, 24 – 25).
3) Og (Psalm 135:11).
4) Zero.
5) Samson (Judges 15:15 – 19).
6) Faith (2 Timothy 4:7).

Score Correct_____ Date_____ Name _____
Study Notes:_____
_____

Quiz 185

1) Is the book of Joel in the Old Testament, the New Testament, or neither?
2) Who did Ezekiel charge was more corrupt in all her ways than her elder sister Samaria and younger sister Sodom?
   Succoth, Zaphon, Gerasa, Jerusalem
3) In 2 Kings, who healed the waters of Jericho by casting salt into a spring?
   Isaiah, Elisha, Jeremy, Habakkuk
4) Who awakened out his sleep and said, "Surely the Lord is in this place."?
   Jacob, David, Solomon, Stephen
5) Who was Saul's father?
   Jonathan, Michal, Goliath, Kish
6) Which weapon is not mentioned in 2 Chronicles 26, which described Uzziah's armory for his soldiers?
   Swords, spears, bows, slings

ANSWERS:

1) Old Testament. (Joel is the twenty-ninth book of the Old Testament.)
2) Jerusalem (Ezekiel 16:2 – 3, 46 – 47).
3) Elisha (2 Kings 2:18 – 22).
4) Jacob (Genesis 28:16).
5) Kish (1 Samuel 9:1 – 2).
6) Swords (2 Chronicles 26:13 – 14).

Score Correct _____ Date _____ Name _____

Study Notes: _____

_____

Quiz 186

1) Is the book of Proverbs in the Old Testament, the New Testament, or neither?

2) When Jesus called Lazarus out from the grave, Lazarus emerged wrapped in grave clothes while his face was bound about with a _____?
Rope, pillow, vine, napkin

3) From Psalm 23: "Thou preparest a table before me in the presence of _____."
My Father, mine enemies, divine creation, my loved ones

4) What king of Israel claimed to worship the false god, Baal, only to destroy the worshippers of Baal?
Ahab, Jehu, Elah, Pekah

5) Whose mother-in-law was Naomi and sister-in-law Ruth?
Deborah, Orpah, Adah, Rizpah

6) Fill in the blank from Genesis 1: "In the beginning God created the _____ and the earth."
Heavens, Word, spirit, heaven

ANSWERS:

1) Old Testament. (Proverbs is the twentieth book of the Old Testament.)

2) Napkin (John 11:43 – 44).

3) Mine enemies (Psalm 23:5).

4) Jehu (2 Kings 10:18 – 25).

5) Orpah (Ruth 1:3 – 6).

6) Heaven (Genesis 1:1).

Score Correct_____ Date_____ Name _____
Study Notes:_____
_____

Quiz 187

1) Is the book of Jeremiah in the Old Testament, the New Testament, or neither?
2) Who said, "I will wipe Jerusalem as a man wipeth a dish, wiping it, and turning it upside down," because of all the evil they had done?
   David, the Lord, Solomon, Hezekiah
3) What was Zedekiah's original name?
   Eutychus, Mattaniah, Cain, Ethbaal
4) From Revelation: "Unto every man that heareth the words of the prophecy of this book, if any man shall add unto these things, God shall add unto him the _____ that are written in this book."
   Hardships, plagues, sorrows, torments
5) Who ran into a congregation carrying incense to stop a plague?
   Moses, Aaron, Izhar, Anak
6) Michal was given as a wife to David after he brought in how many Philistine foreskins as a gift to her father?
   Twenty-five, fifty, one hundred, two hundred

ANSWERS:

1) Old Testament. (Jeremiah is the twenty-fourth book of the Old Testament.)
2) The Lord (2 Kings 21:12 – 15).
3) Mattaniah (2 Kings 24:17).
4) Plagues (Revelation 22:18).
5) Aaron (Numbers 16:46 – 47).
6) Two hundred (1 Samuel 18:27).

Score Correct_____ Date_____ Name _____

Study Notes: _____

_____

Quiz 188

1) Is the book of Jehoash in the Old Testament, the New Testament, or neither?

2) When Ezekiel was lifted up by a spirit taking him between earth and heaven, what part of Ezekiel was the spirit holding on to? Hand, waist, legs, lock of hair

3) To whom did Paul address, "Mine own son after the common faith."? Timothy, Philemon, Titus, James

4) From Proverbs: "All the ways of a man are clean in his own eyes; but the Lord weigheth the _____." Heart, soul, spirits, truth

5) Who was exiled to the land of Nod? Cain, Abel, Abraham, Aaron

6) In the Lord's Prayer, what is God asked to give us that represents the basic needs of the day? Forgiveness of debts, thy kingdom come, love for one another, our daily bread

ANSWERS:

1) Neither. (Jehoash was a king of Judah and a different Jehoash was a king of Israel.)

2) Lock of hair (Ezekiel 8:1 – 3).

3) Titus (Titus 1:1 – 4).

4) Spirits (Proverbs 16:2).

5) Cain (Genesis 4:14 – 16).

6) Our daily bread (Matthew 6:9 – 11).

Score Correct_____ Date_____ Name _____
Study Notes:_____
_____

Quiz 189

1) Is the book of Miriam in the Old Testament, the New Testament, or neither?

2) What piece of war equipment was invented by Uzziah's men?
   Bulwarks, habergeons, battering rams, engines

3) Jesus told his brethren that the world hated him because he said its works were _____?
   Ungodly, evil, greedy, warring

4) In the book of Jeremiah, when God promised to rebuild Israel, he reminded them he had loved with what kind of love?
   Fatherly, everlasting, brotherly, unselfish

5) Ahab, as king of Israel, reigned in what place for twenty and two years?
   Canaan, Ramah, Samaria, Nubia

6) What visual aid did Jesus use on answering the disciples' question, "Who is the greatest in the kingdom of heaven"?
   Sea, ant, leper, child

ANSWERS:

1) Neither. (Miriam was the elder sister of Moses.)

2) Engines (To shoot arrows and great stones; 2 Chronicles 26:14 – 15).

3) Evil (John 7:3 – 7).

4) Everlasting (Jeremiah 31:1 – 4).

5) Samaria (1 Kings 16:28 – 29).

6) Child (Matthew 18:1 – 4).

Score Correct _____ Date _____ Name _____

Study Notes: _____

_____

Quiz 190

1) Is the book of James in the Old Testament, the New Testament, or neither?

2) When Jesus cleared the temple of merchants, he responded to the Jews asking for a sign of authority by saying, "this temple, and in three days I will raise it up."
Burn, crush, destroy, drown

3) What did Jesus classify as the "leaven of the Pharisees"?
Hypocrisy, gluttony, unbelief, lust

4) What did Abraham call the name of the place where he offered up a ram as a burnt offering instead of sacrificing his son Isaac?
Osroene, Ramathlehi, Machpela, Jehovahjireh

5) According to Proverbs, what is it better to get than gold?
A mate, health, wisdom, salvation

6) To whom did God say to be fruitful, and multiply, and replenish the earth?
The Israelites, Adam and Eve, Hebrews, Noah and his wife

ANSWERS:

1) New Testament. (James is the twentieth book of the New Testament.)

2) Destroy (He spake of the temple of his body. John 2:16 – 21).

3) Hypocrisy (Luke 12:1).

4) Jehovahjireh (Genesis 22:9 – 14).

5) Wisdom (Proverbs 16:16).

6) Adam and Eve (Genesis 1:27 – 28).

Score Correct_____ Date_____ Name _____
Study Notes: _____
_____

Quiz 191

1) Is the book of Jonathan in the Old Testament, the New Testament, or neither?

2) After Belshazzar the king of the Chaldeans was slain, who took his kingdom?
   Bethuel the Syrian, Darius the Median, Cyrus the Persian, Raguel the Midianite

3) What was Jehoiakim's original name?
   Jedidiah, Eliakim, Laban, Ahaziah

4) In which book does it say Jesus keeps numbered the very hairs of your head?
   Matthew, Mark, Hebrews, Jude

5) Who said the Bible's shortest prayer when he cried, "Lord, save me."?
   Jonah, Daniel, Peter, James

6) What animal is described in the Bible as eating grass like an ox, moving its tail like a cedar, and having bones like bars of iron?
   Leviathan, pygarg, ossifrage, behemoth

ANSWERS:

1) Neither. (Jonathan was the eldest son of king Saul and a close friend of David.)
2) Darius the Median (Daniel 5:30 – 31).
3) Eliakim (2 Chronicles 36:4).
4) Matthew (Matthew 10:30).
5) Peter (Matthew 14:29 – 30).
6) Behemoth (Job 40:15 – 24).

Score Correct_____ Date_____ Name _____

Study Notes: _____

_____

Quiz 192

1) Is the book of Lehi in the Old Testament, the New Testament, or neither?
2) Fill in the blank (using the same word) from 1 Corinthians: "When I was a _____, I spake as a _____, I understood as a _____, I thought as a _____; but when I became a man, I put away _____ish things."
   Fool, child, brute, sheep
3) What can one do to the devil, so he will flee from you?
   Argue, yell, swear, resist
4) How long did Ezekiel lie upon his left side to bear the iniquity of the house of Israel?
   Seven hours, 127 hours, seven times seven days, 390 days
5) What king of Tyre supplied logs to Solomon to build the Lord's temple?
   Neco, Zelophehad, Rezin, Hiram
6) Who escaped Damascus when the disciples took him by night, letting him down a wall in a basket?
   Naboth, David, Saul, Peter

ANSWERS:
1) Neither. (Lehi was a district near Jerusalem where Samson achieved a victory over the Philistines.)
2) Child (1 Corinthians 13:11).
3) Resist (James 4:7).
4) 390 days (Ezekiel 4:4 – 5).
5) Hiram (1 Kings 5:8).
6) Saul (Acts 9:22 – 26).

Score Correct_____ Date_____ Name _____
Study Notes: _____
_____

Quiz 193

1) Is the book of Magi in the Old Testament, the New Testament, or neither?
2) Where did God select three hundred men among Gideon's troops to fight the Midianites?
   Well of Harod, Sea of Galilee, Well of Sirah, River Jordan
3) Who tried to take a well at Beersheba away from Abraham?
   Abimelech, Samson, Ezekiel, Pekahiah
4) What were the rings (rims) of the four wheels in Ezekiel's vision full of?
   Eyes, hands, tongues, fire
5) Where did Elijah bring a widow's son back to life?
   Smyrna, Corinth, Sardis, Zarephath
6) According to Proverbs, what type of heart doeth good like a medicine?
   Warm, beating, merry, young

ANSWERS:
1) Neither. (Magi are often referred to as the Wise Men who visited Jesus after his birth.)
2) Well of Harod (Judges 7:1 – 7).
3) Abimelech (Genesis 21:22 – 32).
4) Eyes (Ezekiel 1:16 – 18).
5) Zarephath (1 Kings 17:9 – 23).
6) Merry (Proverbs 17:22).

Score Correct _____ Date _____ Name _____

Study Notes: _____

_____

Quiz 194

1) Is the book of Nebo in the Old Testament, the New Testament, or neither?

2) On his deathbed, who told his son to "keep the charge of the Lord thy God, to walk in his ways, to keep his statutes, and his commandments, and his judgments, and his testimonies."?
   Adam, David, Abraham, Zechariah

3) In the book of Revelation, what were the three unclean spirits like?
   Fire, serpents, frogs, death

4) In the book of Acts, whose name is interpreted as the "son of consolation"?
   Immanuel, Peter, Paul, Barnabas

5) Who were the Hebrew midwives at the time of Moses' birth?
   Puah and Shiprah, Merab and Joanna, Zillah and Michal, Jael and Abi

6) Which tribe of Israel had the responsibility for moving the Ark of the Covenant?
   Gad, Dan, Levi, Asher

ANSWERS:

1) Neither. (Mount Nebo is now in western Jordan and was from where Moses viewed the Promised Land of Canaan.)

2) David to Solomon (1 Kings 2:1 – 3).

3) Frogs (Revelation 16:13).

4) Barnabas (Acts 4:36).

5) Puah and Shiprah (Exodus 1:15).

6) Levi (Deuteronomy 10:8).

Score Correct _____ Date _____ Name _____

Study Notes: _____

Quiz 195

1) Is the book of Shekel in the Old Testament, the New Testament, or neither?
2) Jesus said, "A prophet is not without honour, save in his own _____, and in his own _____."
   Flock/valley, country/house, beliefs/sanctuary, church/congregation
3) When Abraham dwelled between Kadesh and Shur, where did he sojourn?
   Gerar, Nimrod, Aj, Tarsus
4) How many times is "daisy" specifically mentioned as a plant in the Bible?
   Zero, three, seven, dozens of times
5) Where did Elisha visit Benhadad, a sick king of Syria?
   Damascus, Nazareth, Salamis, Neapolis
6) The phrase "Praise ye the Lord" begins and ends which five consecutive Psalms?
   1 – 5, 63 – 67, 75 – 79, 146 – 150

ANSWERS:

1) Neither. (Shekel is the standard monetary unit of modern Israel that dates back to ancient weights and coins of the biblical era.)
2) Country/house (Matthew 13:57).
3) Gerar (Genesis 20:1).
4) Zero.
5) Damascus (2 Kings 8:7).
6) 146 – 150 (Psalms 146 – 150 begin and end "Praise ye the Lord").

Score Correct _____ Date _____ Name _____
Study Notes: _____
_____

Quiz 196

1) Is the book of Tigris in the Old Testament, the New Testament, or neither?
2) According to Philippians, one should forget about the things behind them and press toward the mark for the _____ of the high calling of God.
   Salvation, forgiveness, house, prize
3) How many days did the children of Israel weep for Moses' death?
   Two, thirty, fifty, one hundred
4) Who was Barnabas sent to Tarsus to bring back, and on finding brought him to Antioch?
   Mark, Peter, John the Baptist, Saul
5) Jesus said that if you love him to keep his _____?
   Words, commandments, followers, beliefs
6) Whose "eyes stand out with fatness" in Psalm 73?
   Demons, the wicked, serpents, the unholy

ANSWERS:
1) Neither. (Hiddekel was one of the rivers of Paradise with its modern name being Tigris.)
2) Prize (Philippians 3:13 – 14).
3) Thirty (Deuteronomy 34:8).
4) Saul (Acts 11:25 – 26).
5) Commandments (John 14:15).
6) The wicked (Psalm 73:7 – 12).

Score Correct_____ Date_____ Name _____

Study Notes: _____

_____

Quiz 197

1) Is the book of Titus in the Old Testament, the New Testament, or neither?
2) When Moses neared the burning bush, what did God tell him he was standing on?
   The streets of Jerusalem, holy ground, fields of glory, righteous earth
3) How many perished when the tower in Siloam fell?
   Twelve, eighteen, twenty, forty
4) The Lord admonishes people who only honor him with what part of their body?
   Lips, mind, hands, lower
5) What sin did Paul tell the Thessalonians was likely to occur at night?
   Thievery, idolizing, adultery, drunkenness
6) According to Proverbs, the wicked have to do "what" to sleep well?
   Lie, mischief, sin, frown

ANSWERS:
1) New Testament. (Titus is the seventeenth book of the New Testament.)
2) Holy ground (Exodus 3:3 – 5).
3) Eighteen (Luke 13:4).
4) Lips (Isaiah 29:13).
5) Drunkenness (1 Thessalonians 5:7).
6) Mischief (Proverbs 4:14 – 16).

Score Correct_____ Date_____ Name _____
Study Notes:_____

_____

Quiz 198

1) Is the book of John in the Old Testament, the New Testament, or neither?
2) From the book of 1 Samuel, how many boys did Jesse, that Ephrathite of Bethlehemjudah, have?
   Four, eight, eleven, fourteen
3) With two different biblical answers, who was the father of Joseph (wife of Mary)?
   Jacob/Heli, Gideon/Ishmael, Solomon/Nahum, Samuel/Pilate
4) Who shut the mouths of the lions as Daniel was delivered from the den with no matter of hurt found upon him?
   Guard, prisoner, Melzar, angel
5) How many books of the Bible begin with the letter "Z"?
   Zero, one, two, three
6) From what type of tree did Solomon make harps and psalteries (stringed instruments) for singers?
   Fig, cypress, cedar, algum

ANSWERS:
1) New Testament. (John is the fourth book of the New Testament.)
2) Eight (1 Samuel 17:12).
3) Jacob/Heli (Jacob: Matthew 1:16; Heli: Luke 3:23).
4) Angel (Daniel 6:21 – 23).
5) Two (The Old Testament books of Zephaniah and Zechariah).
6) Algum (2 Chronicles 9:10 – 11).

Score Correct _____ Date _____ Name _____
Study Notes: _____

_____

Quiz 199

1) Is the book of Jezebel in the Old Testament, the New Testament, or neither?
2) Who (in addition to Moses) did God ask, "How long shall I bear with this evil congregation which murmur against me"?
   Adam, Aaron, Noah, David
3) Which of these musical instruments were *not* played before the Lord by David and all the house of Israel?
   Psalteries, timbrels, cornets, sackbuts
4) How many talents of gold, among other valuables, did the Queen of Sheba give Solomon?
   Two, fifty, one hundred, one hundred and twenty
5) Who was the first human being to experience physical death?
   Adam, Abel, Aaron, Abraham
6) In Exodus 23, what did God command his people to do on the seventh day, as on six days thou shalt do thy work?
   Worship, sing, visit, rest

ANSWERS:

1) Neither. (Jezebel, daughter of Ethbaal, was a queen known for associating with false prophets.)
2) Aaron (Numbers 14:26 – 27).
3) Sackbuts (2 Samuel 6:5).
4) 120 (2 Chronicles 9:9).
5) Abel (Genesis 4:8).
6) Rest (Exodus 23:12).

Score Correct_____ Date_____ Name _____
Study Notes: _____
_____

Quiz 200

1) Is the book of Jordan in the Old Testament, the New Testament, or neither?

2) When a soldier pierced Jesus' side with a spear after he was crucified on the cross, forthwith came there out blood and _____?
   Holy Ghost, wisps of smoke, two doves, water

3) In which book do you find the find the phrase, "God is love"?
   Genesis, Nehemiah, Hebrews, 1 John

4) Who did Jesus tell that if he had any power against him at all, it had been given to him from above?
   Pilate, Satan, Herod, Legion

5) Which king had admirers of women purified with sweet odours?
   Ahasuerus, Eglon, Josiah, Manasseh

6) According to the book of Romans, what should be a living sacrifice?
   Demons, elders, our bodies, our enemies

ANSWERS:

1) Neither. (Jordan River or the River Jordan is in western Asia and where Jesus was baptized by John the Baptist.)

2) Water (John 19:33 – 34. Writers later labeled that spear the "Spear of Destiny").

3) 1 John (Twice: 4:8, 16).

4) Pilate (John 19:10 – 11).

5) Ahasuerus (Esther 2:12).

6) Our bodies (Romans 12:1).

Score Correct _____ Date _____ Name _____

Study Notes: _____

_____

Quiz 201

1) Is the book of Ezekiel in the Old Testament, the New Testament, or neither?

2) As revealed unto him by the Holy Ghost, who would not see death before seeing the Lord's Christ?
Caiaphas, Simeon, Annas, Maath

3) How many times does the word "Easter" appear in the Bible?
Zero, one, three, seventeen

4) In the book of Hebrews, who was the King of righteousness?
Neco, Joash, Melchisedec, Zechariah

5) Who was Judas Iscariot the son of?
Satan, Simon, Sisera, Solomon

6) What is the last word in the book of Revelation, thus the last word in the Bible?
Amen, grace, salvation, all

ANSWERS:

1) Old Testament. (Ezekiel is the twenty-sixth book of the Old Testament.)

2) Simeon (Luke 2:25 – 26).

3) One (Acts 12:4).

4) Melchisedec (Hebrews 7:1 – 2).

5) Simon (John 6:71).

6) Amen (Revelation 22:21).

Score Correct _____ Date_____ Name _____
Study Notes: _____
_____

The Last Judgment

Acknowledgments

Whenever there is a roll call of ones who made this work possible, there are always ones who are inadvertently left out. I apologize for that and will always cherish their hospitality, wise counsel, and genuine friendship. But to the ones listed and to any left out, I can only reciprocate but never repay. However, I do sincerely thank certain persons and mediums whose unsung contributions to my work were very specific.

Lord God Almighty: The continued inspiration in my life
The Holy Bible: King James Version utilized in my research
Rita Rosenkranz: My literary agent and business partner, NYC
Joseph Craig: Skyhorse Publishing (Good Books) editor on project, NYC
Clipart.ChristiansUnite.com: Illustrations utilized throughout

Proofreaders and Sounding Board:
Shirley Blaes, Spartanburg, SC
Deane Brown, Spartanburg, SC
Fran L. Burgess, Woodruff, SC
Judy Cathcart Calvert, Union, SC
Anne H. Campbell, Sumter, SC
Casey Campbell, Sumter, SC
Colleen Casey, Spartanburg, SC
Shannon Creighton, Spartanburg, SC
Eric and Bryn Douglass, West Columbia, SC
Joyce Finkle, Spartanburg, SC

Zan and Louise Fisher, Spartanburg, SC
Paul Harmon, Spartanburg, SC
Tony Keller, Westerly, RI
Kelli C. Lanford, Boiling Springs, SC
Wayne Major, Cowpens, SC
Larry Morton, Winterville, NC
Linda Norton, Pawcatuck, CT
Lila Floyd Price, Spartanburg, SC
Bruton Redding, Spartanburg, SC
Sean Sabo, Allentown, PA
Jeanette G. Simpkins, Woodruff, SC
Rocky Simpkins, Woodruff, SC
Chief Clary and Martha Sprouse, Spartanburg, SC
Steve M. Whitaker, Spartanburg, SC
Jean Wilson, Enoree, SC
Neal Woods, Spartanburg, SC

And to any/all others inadvertently omitted, my sincere thanks.

Index

Eglon, 169
Ehud, 147, 152, 170
Ekron, 65
Elah, 130
Elam, 36
Eleazar, 136
Eli, 46, 68, 89, 100, 166
Eliab, 56
Elijah, 104, 106, 118, 119, 122, 135, 186, 206
Eliphaz, 30
Elisabeth, 91
Elisha, 67, 93, 198, 208
Elkanah, 55
Elymas, 112, 122
Enoch, 23, 85, 106
Ephesians, Book of, 26, 42, 95, 111, 129, 159, 170
Ephesus, 33, 139
Ephraim, 58
Ephrath, 111
Esau, Book of, 41
Esther, Book of, 11, 35, 61, 62, 95, 109, 126, 133, 134, 140, 169, 196, 213
Eunice, 54
Euphrates, 12, 37
Eutychus, 73
Eve, 39, 50, 67, 90, 96, 125, 136
Exodus, 8, 9, 16, 17, 20, 21, 25, 28, 33, 34, 37, 43, 46, 51, 57, 58, 67, 68, 69, 85, 87, 89, 95, 108, 113, 114, 119, 123, 129, 139, 142, 144, 145, 150, 153, 159, 162, 166, 175, 177, 187, 207, 210, 212
Ezekiel, 10, 53, 55, 121, 158, 198, 201
Ezekiel, Book of, 10, 53, 55, 95, 130, 140, 158, 160, 182, 188, 205, 206, 214

Ezra, Book of, 10, 35, 95, 103

F
Felix, 12
Festus, 97
1 Chronicles, 26, 35, 41, 44, 52, 66, 122, 126, 151, 158, 182, 193
1 Corinthians, 18, 22, 41, 92, 113, 121, 143, 146, 148, 205
1 John, 43, 111, 114, 134, 169, 213
1 Kings, 6, 17, 24, 28, 30, 31, 44, 49, 62, 66, 68, 76, 81, 88, 89, 102, 114, 115, 122, 130, 135, 163, 165, 179, 183, 185, 186, 192, 193, 205, 206, 207
1 Peter, 65, 97, 120, 136, 157, 187
1 Samuel, 29, 45, 46, 55, 56, 57, 59, 68, 70, 80, 89, 100, 105, 109, 117, 125, 132, 134, 141, 164, 166, 171, 174, 178, 179, 180, 185, 191, 193, 198, 200, 211
1 Thessalonians, 13, 67, 100, 210
1 Timothy, 16, 23, 37, 99, 102, 107, 123
Fortunatus, 153

G
Gabriel, 138
Galatia, 143
Galatians, Book of, 22, 37, 55, 126, 175, 179, 181, 183
Galilee, 80, 106
Gamaliel, 82
Gath, 59
Gaza, 155